BACKSTAGE PASS

Also by Paul Stanley

FACE THE MUSIC

PAUL STANLEY

STANLEY

BACKSTAGE PASS

HarperOne
An Imprint of HarperCollins*Publishers*

HarperOne

HarperCollins books may be purchased for educational, business, or sales promotional use. For information, please email the Special Markets Department at SPsales@harpercollins.com.

FIRST EDITION

Designed by SBI Book Arts, LLC

Library of Congress Cataloging-in-Publication Data is available upon request.

ISBN 978-0-06-282028-0
ISBN 978-0-06-295134-2 (BN)
ISBN 978-0-06-295328-5 (BS)

19 20 21 22 23   LSC   10 9 8 7 6 5 4 3 2 1

To my dad, who has saved
his greatest gifts to me for last

CONTENTS

CONTENTS

PART THREE

SELF, HEALTH, AND HAPPINESS

INTRODUCTION

There was a time when I wished my father would die.

Before my mom passed away, my dad was not a nice person. He was really difficult to be around and very angry. So I hoped he wouldn't be around—and that his death would be a quick solution to the ugliness that was happening between my parents and tainting so much around him.

But I'm lucky: in the years since the publication of my first book, *Face the Music*, I've been fortunate enough to get to a point where I can say to my dad, "I wish you could be here forever."

He's going to be ninety-nine, and in these most recent years, rather than being saddled with strictly negative memories, I have been given some things I'll actually miss.

My dad had a hard time reading *Face the Music* because I talked so openly about the misery I experienced as a child, the lack of support I got at home, and the problems between my parents—the constant fighting and lack of affection. Since the book came out, I've found myself sometimes recollecting things with my dad that he doesn't remember—but that were great. He took me to the opera, for instance. And he took me to museums. So although he couldn't connect with me on an emotional level, he still took me places that shaped who I am, the good and the bad.

What I left out of *Face the Music* was the fact that, despite his flaws, my dad was well intentioned. In the past, I regarded that as irrelevant. But now I can see that it did make a difference—and that I can learn from that too.

To try to illustrate this to my dad, I reminded him of the time when I was probably eight or nine years old and asked him for sunglasses. I told him I wanted to buy sunglasses at the luncheonette around the corner from our apartment. And he said, "No, I'll get you *good* sunglasses." So he ordered a pair of quality sunglasses from an optometrist, but unfortunately it backfired, because when I saw them, I hated them. I've sat with him since *Face the Music* came out and said, "Remember, you bought me good glasses."

The process that made our relationship ultimately so much better was setting boundaries, which creates a level of self-respect and respect for other people. We can't allow somebody to make a fool of us or lower our self-worth or treat us less than we believe is acceptable. It's fine to set the rules for interactions: let someone know what is acceptable and what isn't. That's not sitting down when we meet somebody and reading them the riot act. It happens through their seeing how we deal with situations with others and how we deal with situations with them. I've said all of this to my adult son, Evan, and I believe it's very important.

Initially my parents were thrown by the idea that I could say something to them that they thought was unacceptable, or that I could hang up the phone on my father when I thought he was out of line. He would call me back and say, "You hung up on me!" And I would say, "Yeah, I told you that talking to me like that is not acceptable."

It's important in all relationships to preserve and protect our self-respect.

Even so, I'm a strong advocate of leaving as little to regret as possible. As my life has progressed, I've always wanted to make sure that I didn't have coulda-shoulda-woulda scenarios left on my plate. I would rather hash these things out. Seeing my dad at ninety-eight means that every day is unknown and precarious. For both of our benefit, it's not a time to leave things unsaid.

Talking with my dad about his demise is addressing the elephant in the room. It's no secret to him that his days are numbered. He has an almost contradictory outlook about that: he says he's lived too long and all the people he knew have died. To which I reply, "They'd all change places with you." But when he's not well, he makes sure he goes to the hospital and then says, "Boy, that was close."

So on one hand, he says he shouldn't be here, but on the other hand, on some level he wants to be here.

There's so much to be lost by not talking about mortality. And in the course of the conversations I've had with him about it, I realized I needed to tell him that his grandchildren will miss him, and as basic and as childish as it sounds, I needed to tell him that I will miss him too. That I will miss him and that I wish he could stay forever.

The night before I decided to first broach this topic with my dad, I thought I had to talk to him tomorrow because I didn't know how many tomorrows we had left. The change in our relationship needed to be acknowledged. So I told him, "You know, I'll miss you."

Which is a terrific change. I couldn't have said that to him five years ago, because five years ago I wasn't rooting for him. But I needed to say it, and I didn't want to end up thinking what so many people in similar situations think after it's too late: *I wish I'd told him when I'd had the chance.*

I did have the chance, and I wanted to use it.

That's something really cool about this chapter of my life. Not that our conversations erase the past, but rather than being left with a lot of bitterness or bad memories, I enjoy being around the person my dad has become. And he's learned to be supportive. I feel very fortunate.

And I guess it ties in to the other thing I've learned: that my dad will continue on. Yes, I will remember the things that weren't so great, but I will also remember the fact that we came to terms with each other. That's a good thing. That's a great thing.

That's a gift.

My dad is a much nicer person—still haunted by his demons, still haunted by guilt, but nice and kind. Setting boundaries for other people allows us to decide what is acceptable and what isn't. And my verbalizing my boundaries to my father, making clear to him what is acceptable and what isn't, was probably the start of the transformation between us. These days my dad is very supportive and comes out to see my musical side project, Soul Station. He wants to know how the shows go and how my art exhibitions go. He compliments me on things I do. And it doesn't matter how old we are; everybody wants their parents' approval.

In the past, my dad's acknowledgment of my accomplishments, if I ever got any, was always tinged with jealousy and resentment. To have it without that is a blessing, because his life is—he knows and I know—coming to an end.

So I'm blessed.

I'm blessed that I can tell him that I love him, that I'll miss him. It's something I didn't expect, and it's something I didn't have before and didn't have when I wrote *Face the Music*. It's a good thing.

I don't want my dad to die. Now I'm lucky enough to be able to tell him that I wish he *wouldn't* die and I wish he could always be here. It's a gift to him, but it's probably a bigger gift to me, because I'm going to remain. I've tied up the loose ends.

The end of *Face the Music* feels like the end. But it's never the end. There's always a new end. And a new beginning.

Finding both is what this book is about. If you're young and envisioning a new path forward that will lead you to a better end, or you're farther along in years and looking to reimagine a different future, this book is an all-access pass to what I've learned. I hope it serves you well.

Who doesn't long for the mythical backstage pass? In rock and roll, the backstage pass is the golden ticket. It's the pass that allows you to see what most people never get a chance to see—the inner workings; the pass that allows you to see behind the curtain and glimpse the true Wizard of Oz. The backstage pass allows you to see all the dedication and debauchery that is everyone's fantasy. But how real is that fantasy?

In life we often yearn for something and seek it out, only to be surprised by the reality. But therein lies the gift. Everything isn't always as it appears, and reality can be far more life changing than our fantasy.

You now hold in your hands that backstage pass, a chance to finally see the good, the bad, and the ugly—and hopefully to be that much wiser for it.

This book spells out my approach to success and living the good life. It's an approach to being healthier in mind and body, to having a more fulfilled and rewarding life. And you don't even have to put on a Yoda outfit.

Of course, the good life looks different for different people. For some, it might mean laughing more with their kids; for others, it's a nice glass of Italian wine. And while I enjoy both of those things, the specifics don't matter. It's about an approach to life. And this approach has worked for me.

The lessons I've learned—contained in this book—are truths. But I'm not here to tell you this is the path to success. I'm here to tell you that you can find your own path to success—that it's in you. Everybody has a destiny or destination they can pursue and reach, or not. So I'm not here to lecture anybody; I'm here to cheerlead. I'm here to explain what I did and how—and how *you* can too.

Of course, it would be presumptuous of me to tell you how to deal with your personal life. After all, I've never lived a day as you have. All I can do is tell you what I've done and hope that serves as a road map or a template to help you discover who you are. I didn't have a road map, and as a result I made a lot of mistakes. I got a lot out of those mistakes, but I can spare you from making the same ones so you can set up an effective plan of your own.

I'm not a therapist. I'm not a bodybuilder. I'm not a dietician. But I don't think self-improvement is rocket science. With a little bit of guidance and a little bit of support, we can do it together.

I'm also not here to tell you to do anything you don't want to do—after all, the only person we have the potential to change is ourselves. But I'm here to do it with you, to serve as a guide. I'm here to show you how you can establish an effective outlook that will influence every aspect of your life.

One thing I've found—and a thing that's humbling for somebody who believes he can change most anything—is that I can't change other people. So this isn't about *me* changing you. This is about *you* changing you.

And if you want to change, you can.

PART ONE

BUSINESS AND SUCCESS

1

LET THE PAST
BE THE PAST

Last spring, I returned to West 211th Street, in Upper Manhattan, to the one-bedroom apartment where I grew up. It hadn't been a happy home, to put it mildly. I hadn't been in that building in sixty years. I'd driven by it once or twice, and I hadn't had a good feeling when I did.

This time, I had a specific reason to go there: along with my wife, Erin, and my oldest son, Evan, my three younger children—Colin, age twelve, Sarah, age ten, and Emily, age seven—were with me, and I wanted them to see the place where I'd started my life. I hoped it would help them understand the difference between their lives and mine.

Years ago I had visited the area in Queens where my family moved when we left Upper Manhattan. Queens is where I lived when I went to high school, started playing music, met a bass player named Gene Simmons, and eventually started KISS. But after that visit, I fell into a few weeks of feeling miserable. It sort of confirmed what I had always thought: these places from my past held only negative associations for me.

Still, I thought it was important to give it another try. I hoped this visit to 211th Street would offer a beautiful chance to give concrete reality to the stories I've told my kids over the years, to make my childhood memories into something tangible for them.

So we went back. Or, I should say, I went back, since they'd never been there.

I was born with a crumpled mass of cartilage instead of a right ear, a facial difference known as microtia. From the time I can remember, people stared at me—both kids and adults. People seem to detach a deformity from the person—instead of being treated like a human being, I was treated like an object. An object of curiosity in some cases, I guess, but most often an object of disgust.

When I started to attend the elementary school right next door to our apartment, PS 98, I didn't have any friends, but I was always the center of attention. And that sort of attention felt just horrific to a five-year-old. I wanted to disappear. Or hide. But there was no place to go.

It was one thing when somebody stared at me—that was bad enough. But when someone yelled out at me, that drew other people's eyes to me—everyone would look at me, scrutinize me. I felt violated and threatened to my core. These were the worst moments—like the kid who would point and yell, "Stanley, the one-eared monster!"

All I could think was: *You're hurting me.*

14

On top of that, I never had a shoulder to cry on. My parents insisted on not talking about it. Kids need parents. Kids need protection. When my parents didn't empathize with me and didn't want to hear about my problems, I felt cut off from everybody.

For most of my life, West 211th Street had represented just one thing for me: pain.

But now, as I drove up toward the apartment, I wondered whether it would be different.

We arrived and walked through the entry arch to the five-story walk-up and stepped into a paved space surrounded by the building—to call it a courtyard would make it sound too nice. Memories started to rush back. Crossing the yard, I suddenly remembered jumping on another kid's back and biting him. This kid had taunted me and spat in my face. The courtyard triggered the memory because I'd been there one day with my mom and explained to her that this kid had been bullying me and hinted that I might want or need her help dealing with the situation. And she had told me, a kindergartner, to fight my own battles.

"Don't come crying to me," she said.

Which led to my attacking the kid.

Entering the apartment, my initial reaction was surprise at how small the place was. Obviously, when we remember something in one scale—based on our size and stature as a child—and we go back, it's startling. The building was also a bit rundown, but it was the size that really surprised me. As small as I remember it, this was so much smaller. And four of us had lived in it—my parents, my sister, and me. My parents had slept in the living room on a foldout sofa, and if my sister or I got up earlier than them and wanted to go to the kitchen, we had to crawl under their bed.

My heart was racing. I was a bit light-headed.

Back outside, we saw the school next door, and the schoolyard where I'd been called "Stanley, the one-eared monster."

I've always told my kids to remember that their dad was teased and ridiculed. I've always told them that it hurt me and that they should remember, when dealing with other people, how I had been a target. That means a lot to them, and I see its impact in their eyes. Colin is aware of others' vulnerabilities, as is Sarah. Even Emily is keenly aware of the feelings of others. If it happened to their dad, it could happen to anybody.

And it does, though during my childhood it never occurred to me that I might not be the only one to be bullied and to suffer. Children tend not to think in terms of how they fit into the wider world. I never thought about anyone else being taunted and bullied because my world was just me. And even if somebody else was being subjected to similar treatment, it didn't matter—I was still hurting. I wouldn't have been consoled knowing that somebody else was also getting beaten up.

My children all know about my being stared at and pointed at, about my having trouble in school and not being able to hear—all kinds of adversity. It's the best way for them to really understand that sort of thing, to attach a face to it: *my* face. A face that, as a member of their family, probably means the most to them.

But now, standing there in that apartment and schoolyard more than sixty years later, all of it felt like another lifetime. The memories were still there, but my connection to the place no longer had negative overtones. I could tell that, unlike earlier visits to places in my past, this one wasn't going to leave a mark. It wasn't going to cause pain or bitterness.

That has everything to do with who I have become. And by that I don't mean a globe-trotting rock star with a fancy house and a fancy car. I achieved that fairly early in my life and have realized it didn't help smooth over the emotional scars. At one time I thought a Playboy Playmate and a bankbook full of cash was the answer. But it wasn't. I had wanted so desperately to rub my fame in the faces of cruel classmates at reunions, but it didn't help me feel better. I had wanted so badly to be desired by the sort of women who had always ignored me, but I found I still couldn't establish meaningful relationships. I had wanted so badly to surround myself with the trappings of success, but I found that stuff was still just stuff, no matter the price tag. On the one hand, I had accomplished everything I had ever wanted and more. But on the other, I still languished emotionally, never entirely comfortable with myself, never entirely happy.

The beauty of success is that it has given me the potential to realize a quest: to be the best me. But who I've become is different from who I thought I would become.

And the reason why this visit to my childhood apartment was different from previous glimpses into my past was that when your life is in order, the chaos that you may have been through recedes and becomes irrelevant. I was once much more connected to those times and my struggles in that place. Yet now I was back there with none of that baggage.

I felt some of the same emotions I felt when talking to my dad in recent years about the changes in our relationship. That place—211th Street—may have been where I started, but it wasn't where I ended up, literally and figuratively.

In some strange way, the place now seemed oddly beautiful—because of my sense of perspective, because I could see how far I had come. And again, I don't mean materially. I can now appreciate my past for the same reason I could finally write my story in *Face the Music*, and for the same reason my relationships with people like my father have continued to evolve since that book came out. We keep secrets when we haven't come to terms with the past. We are in turmoil when we haven't come to terms with our feelings. But once we are comfortable, we are freed by letting go.

Going back to 211th Street was a terrific opportunity, a moment of clarity.

When our lives correlate with being in a good place, I realized, then we're ready to unveil difficult things, because they're not the same burden they once were. We may have been unwilling victims in the past, but we can choose whether to allow that past to make us victims in the present and future.

I often hear people express the idea that living well is the best revenge. But I don't know. If we're living well, we shouldn't need revenge. If we still feel that need, then maybe we're not living so well after all. Living well, at this stage in my life, means not needing revenge, not even *wanting* revenge.

But then again, who really knows what it means to live well, at least in advance? For most of my life, I sure didn't. It was something I had to learn—the hard way, and over a long period of time.

The thing is, life doesn't come with an instruction manual. So over the years I've created my own. I've spent a lifetime adding hard-earned principles to this instruction manual, and in following it, I've achieved not only traditional success but also the peace of mind that allows me to see things in a different light. Up to now, that manual existed only in my head, but I decided to turn it into a reality in order to share it, to unveil it as a result of feeling unburdened by my past.

2

BE TOUGH ON YOURSELF, BUT ALWAYS BE YOUR OWN BIGGEST FAN

Growing up the way I did, I reached a point where I realized that patterning myself on the most obvious role models—my parents—was a dead end and would only lead to my downfall in one way or another. So I had to go back to square one and learn. I had to learn to walk again in a philosophical sense, because I hadn't learned how to do it in a healthy way the first time around.

That was my struggle.

I don't say that for sympathy. I say that because we all have challenges.

In my case, in addition to normal kid stuff, I faced the cruelty that comes with a physical difference and the ignorance back then about certain disabilities. Because I was deaf in one ear, I had trouble hearing in school; but instead of getting special help, I was simply dismissed as a bad student and sent to remedial classes. And through it all, my family failed to provide any sense of support. Well, to be honest, it was worse than that. Often my parents made me feel even less secure—to such an extent that I would sleepwalk and have constant nightmares, waking up screaming from dreams that

I now recognize as symbolic: being alone in a speeding car with no steering wheel, being alone on a raft with no way to get to land.

My therapist would say I was abused. Not intentionally, but some of what my parents did was certainly not designed to build me up. I wasn't chained to a chair or anything, but I've also heard that sometimes the less insidious and obvious kinds of abuse can be almost more damaging. So I'm kind of torn. I have to give a disclaimer, but at the same time, I'm aware that anyone can be negatively affected by things that are less overt. A lot of damage can be done in ways that are not so obvious.

I didn't know it as a kid, but my parents weren't happy people. To me, they were just my parents. I assumed that's how adults were.

My way of thinking—ingrained in me at home as a child—was always: don't show pain. Never let anybody know that they hurt you. And of course, because of what I was subjected to as a result of my facial difference, I hurt a lot. I've come to realize that when we pretend not to be hurt, we suffer. It feels better to say, "You hurt me." That allows us to release the pain. It's not a form of weakness, and it doesn't put the person who hurt us in a position of power. It isn't anything more than a statement of fact that we've been hurt. It means nothing more than somebody was cruel or misguided and said something hurtful.

Holding in our hurt, on the other hand, allows a kind of pressure to build up, like in a faucet. At some point the pipe bursts. The key is to keep ourselves open and let it out—keep everything flowing.

At this point in my life, I don't keep things to myself. If somebody says something that hurts me, I tell that person. Nothing else is attached to it. Anything attached to it is either how they choose to see it or how I choose to see it.

If someone who is miserable or full of self-doubt or self-worth issues becomes successful and is still unhappy, that's when they have a choice. Either they give up and give in to unhealthy or even deadly coping mechanisms or they roll up their sleeves and decide *I'm not going to be a victim. I'm going to come through this.* When we choose to be victims, life goes on for everybody else. Maybe early on I saw myself as a victim, but then I realized that I gained nothing by seeing myself that way. And even though the world of rock and roll was full of dangers and temptations, it also seemed obvious to me that burning a hole with cocaine through the cartilage of my septum wasn't going to help anything.

Back then, I navigated life using a lot of preconceived ideas that formed a structure, which I needed. But over time, I found that some of those ideas were just too difficult. A lot of the rules I was living by were based on nothing. It's okay to be tough on ourselves, but when we make rules for ourselves, they have to be based in experience, and my rules were not

realistic. So over a long time I drew up a new set of rules—
the ones in this book.

First I had to unlearn what I'd been taught as a kid. I'd
been programmed to shove everything aside, not to accept
anything that raised questions about what I was doing. If I
didn't talk about something, it didn't exist.

When we're children, in those formative years, we take
our first steps, and not just physically. If our foundation was
faulty when we were young, as it was in my case, we have to
learn to walk again when we're older. I had to build a new foundation. That was difficult. It was like deprogramming. We are,
in essence, programmed by repeated responses or reactions to
things. Only when we start to perceive those things differently, or add new components to how we react to them, can we
deprogram ourselves—and defuse the emotional bomb.

For a long time I took my childhood and my life experiences as the norm. Kids model what they see at home and
think it's normal. And that's how they initially define love,
by what they receive at home and how their parents and sib-
lings treat one another. Once I got enough perspective and
different experience, I woke up to the fact that my childhood
hadn't been the norm. Before a revelation like that, we can't
acknowledge the pain. Supplementing with new life experiences and a new perspective, however, takes the charge out of
painful things from our past. The memory that we were hurt
doesn't go away, but the pain does. And that's an important
distinction. I know how much I hurt for years, even decades,

of my life—I know there was a palpable pain. But the pain is gone because I rectified and remedied my life.

I can acknowledge the hurt, but I no longer feel the pain.

The idea of throwing away what I had been taught, discarding the ways I'd been taught to reason and not to reason—to start again from scratch—was daunting. But I needed to do it. I was driven to cleanse because I felt like what I had seen and what I had emulated was poison and would not make me happy, and life wouldn't end well for me. I was unhappy and unsettled, and I certainly felt despair, but this was part of the quest. Would I live with the decay, or would I get a root canal? Would I dig out the rot or just bear it?

First I had to realize it was okay to question my foundation. After all, my original foundation wasn't making me happy. Second, I realized I could build another foundation—though I also understood this wasn't going to happen overnight. That's why I've always been leery of self-help books and other quick fixes. Going away for a weekend where you don't pee for a couple of days is not going to change your life. You didn't get the way you are in two days, and you're not going to undo it over a weekend either. (Although I should probably also admit that part of what made the process bearable for me was *not* realizing how long it would take.)

Here's the truth: Questioning ourselves is not a weakness. It's a source of strength.

There's great freedom in being able to acknowledge how little we know. There's a cage and handcuffs in thinking we know more than we do. There are shackles in that. Freedom for me came when I admitted I had so much to learn and I knew much less than I'd thought. I'm much happier knowing that many of the things I had thought were, in truth, nonsense. I'd just made them up. I'd made them up because they made me feel secure. But when we're truly secure, we don't need to think we know everything. That's the other part of it. When we feel secure, we don't need all the rules or ideas about what we know, because we're free. We don't need that false sense of support and safety from truisms that aren't true, and that's a release.

I had to ask myself: "How the hell do you have life all sorted out and all worked out?"

I had to start to get healthy before I could realize how my past had affected me. When we think our behavior and how we deal with the world is normal, there's nothing to fix. But when we step away from it, we can say, "Gee, look at all that I'm dealing with and why."

It's confining and suffocating to think we know everything. It's freeing to realize we don't. Maybe everything doesn't need a label. We put "good" and "bad," "true" and "untrue," on things that don't need those grades or categories. Some things just *are*.

We have to take control of our lives.

We don't have to accept who we are today.

We can decide to be someone else tomorrow.

It's not always easy, but we have to have that extra drive, that extra breath, that extra stride that someone else doesn't, to get us where we want to go.

Reaching one goal gives us the opportunity to see another goal. And if we reach a goal and think it's all over, then how sad. Goals reveal a road map to other goals. The most important thing is to keep moving forward. We don't know where we're going to wind up, and we plot a course that may not lead where we think. But if we're going forward, we'll find our destination—and then, if we're lucky, we'll find another one, and another one.

Obstacles are what we see when we lose sight of our goals. If we have to jump hurdles, we jump them. It's about shedding and getting rid of all the baggage and the doubt and the voices in our heads from people around us, and if we're relentless and tireless, we ultimately become a person we can love, a person we can embrace.

Only then do we become the person we were meant to be.

3

EVERY SUCCESS STARTS WITH KNOWING THE DIFFERENCE BETWEEN A DREAM AND A FANTASY

Having big dreams is risky; it's dangerous business. We all had them as children, but for many of us, those dreams died somewhere along the way. In essence, a creative adult is a child who survived.

There is a big difference, however, between dreams and fantasy. Dreams are something that we can accomplish, but only when we know ourselves, our actual gifts and real limitations, and have a passionate plan to get from point A to point B. Fantasy, or magical thinking, on the other hand, is an escape from reality. It's enjoyable—and can even be an important part of the creative process that leads to an achievable dream, like writing a song—but it can also distract us from making real progress.

If we want to succeed, it's important to dream within the realm of the possible—but that doesn't mean what's possible for someone else or what someone else has accomplished. It means intrinsically and innately and honestly knowing what's possible for *ourselves*.

Dreaming becomes the blueprint for reality. Not someone else's reality, but our own.

Self-delusion is self-defeating. I made a conscious decision decades ago not to fool myself. That doesn't mean I saw things accurately, but I wasn't going to deceive myself. The idea of not being honest with oneself is strange to me. I can't understand why people would bullshit themselves. For better or worse, I want to know who I am, what I do, why I do it, and if it needs to change.

My struggle has always been to be the best me. It is ongoing every day. So I've always been hard on myself, and maybe that's the best way to accomplish what's important. Because it's so easy to please other people, but we go home every night and we're the ones who have to live with ourselves. Compliments and attention are pretty hollow and last only as long as another person is talking to us. The core of true success is within. If we stumble into a type of success where others love what we're doing but we don't, that success is fleeting and hollow. The core of enduring success, as in *contentment*, comes from loving what we do—because loving what we do will make us love who we are.

I will say this: the heart has always been the same.

My dream—and the collective dream I shared with Gene, Ace, and Peter back in 1973—started from the premise that we were going to become the biggest rock band around. Of course, that's ridiculous—to many people, including many around us at the time, it didn't seem realistic. But we figured somebody was going to do it—so why not us? why not me?

If we go with the status quo, we tend to live in mediocrity. I was never cut out for that. I always knew that I couldn't work nine to five—it was unthinkable. I would have slit my wrists. Hard work and routine are fine, but that hard work and routine had to be exciting to me—something I had a passion for.

Starting with the notion that KISS was going to succeed and we were going to become big rock stars was not following anybody's safe path. I didn't want to go on somebody's safe path. And anyway, the traditional paths hadn't opened up. All the kids I knew in my neighborhood in Queens became dentists and lawyers. If I'd tried to follow that path, I would have ended up homeless.

Everything changed when I saw the Beatles. Their performance on the *Ed Sullivan Show* in February 1964 changed my life. The August 1964 release of their first movie, *A Hard Day's Night*, also changed the game. I loved the mythology of these four guys who were all for one and one for all. We pictured them all sleeping in the same bed, and the movie offered us a new image of what a band could or should be. The Beatles embodied the idea of four individuals making a band, and you not only loved the band but also loved each individual. As KISS came together, that became our goal as well.

But as far as dreaming big, I never wanted to be the best band on the block. I never wanted to be the best band in the neighborhood. We were keenly aware of the true playing field.

In other words, our goal wasn't to be better than the New York Dolls, who were the hot band in New York City when we were coming up. Our goal was to be as good as our heroes. We refused to judge ourselves on a small scale. Perhaps what helped us succeed was that our vision was far beyond what some of our local competition could conceive.

I hate to use the analogy of the box, but in order to succeed outside the box we have to *see* the box. And not be trapped by it. There's a balance, because we don't want to be limited solely by what we know or don't know. It's a fine line.

I never fooled myself into believing I could do it the same way the Beatles did it, but I was acutely aware throughout my life that I could touch a nerve. The bands and artists I admired set a standard for me to aspire to. I didn't try to imitate them; the influence I was looking for was inspirational, not literal.

Back then, we saw the people who had succeeded—like the Beatles, the Who, or Led Zeppelin—but we didn't necessarily see our competition. We saw the people who were our goal, but not the other contenders. We couldn't see a band in Finland. We couldn't see a band in Dallas. And they couldn't see each other. We saw only the bands we were aspiring to be, but not the other bands that were also aspiring to be them. That had some advantages. It made for individuation. It made for a less homogenous kind of music scene— everybody wasn't just borrowing from one another. Nowadays everybody's aware of everyone else, but that wasn't the case when KISS started out. Until bands got media attention and national or international exposure, they were left to their own devices, and all anyone was aware of were the local bands or the bands they ended up touring with.

When I talk to young bands or young musicians, I sometimes tell them, "If the music you're making isn't of the same standard as that of the bands you love, then you're not good enough. There's only one measuring stick, and that's not the local competition but the top ranks. If you're not up there, you need to keep working. And if you don't want to, then you shouldn't be doing it."

Any great talent right now is keenly aware of their competition—thanks to the internet, it's easier to size up the global arena of competition as opposed to the local competition. And what's happened over the years and decades is that the standard has been upped exponentially, because we're now able to view the world's best from any computer on the planet. A band in Austin knows what a band in Oslo is doing, and vice versa. So being the best singer on your block doesn't cut it.

I really believe that the talent pool has upped its game. The days of *Ted Mack and the Original Amateur Hour*—which was on TV when I was a kid—or even the first generation of national talent shows, like *Star Search*, seem quaint now. What we saw on those shows was just horrendous compared with the level of *The Voice*.

The truth is, back when KISS started, we weren't aware of what was going on around us or around the world. We had no way of gauging ourselves against a broad pool of talent when we were coming up. Now people go on the internet and think, "Geez, I suck."

The internet can be terrific, because the talent that's uncovered is pretty amazing. Whether or not the people succeed ultimately or whether the entertainment is all that survives is another question. But raw ability? If someone is talented and willing to work at it, that person can really raise the bar. The internet also allows people to see who they're up against and be influenced or inspired by that—it's something we simply didn't have when we started KISS.

There's always some mimicry in creative work, and there are now apparently an infinite number of singers out there emulating some of the greats and misguidedly doing vocal runs that border on histrionics. Their vocal stylings often end up more like gymnastics as opposed to being used to communicate emotions. The downside to being able to do all these vocal runs is that it means nothing if there's nothing behind it. Sometimes I hear people singing and I'll say to my wife, Erin, "That person might as well be singing in Mandarin because they have absolutely no clue what they're singing about."

So many elements separate the pretenders from the contenders. Sure, Mariah Carey can sing five octaves or whatever, while Leonard Cohen could sing only half an octave. But time will tell which of their music lives on. It's not what we're capable of doing; it's what we do with our capabilities.

You'll find guys now, unfortunately, who think their favorite blues guitar player is Eddie Van Halen. To do something with depth, with real weight and substance—whether that depth is lost on others—you need roots, you need experience. Someone might say, "Well, KISS is superficial, so who's this guy to be talking?" Well, not superficial to the 100 million people who've bought our albums so they can listen to them over and over. So when I say that roots are essential to whatever you're going to do, I say it in part because I grew up seeing Otis Redding and listening to Dion and the Belmonts and Irving Berlin and Puccini and Jerry Lee Lewis and Muddy Waters, and the list goes on. The point is: it all adds to the stew.

I was a huge Byrds fan. I could play all their songs. I was a fan of Tim Hardin, Phil Ochs, David Blue, the Jim Kweskin Jug Band. I went to the Gaslight down in the Village to see Dave Van Ronk. Those artists may seem superfluous to what I do, but they're all in there. I saw the Temptations. I listened to and watched Jackie Wilson, who was a phenomenal singer and an incredibly magnetic performer. I was a huge fan of Eric Andersen—the idea that, stripped away of everything, someone could sit and mesmerize you with a story or a point of view was a revelation. To hear Eric Andersen sing "Thirsty Boots" was a romantic notion of a different kind of life where somebody incessantly traveled and needed to move; if nothing else, things like that make you aware that there's a whole other world out there. How much of it you want to see is up to you, but I always found that music was a portal into a life that I wasn't part of but on some level wanted to experience.

We can only be as deep as our experiences. We draw from our musical travels, and in my case, even if on the surface some of those places may seem irrelevant, they're all part of it. All the various pieces contribute to a mosaic that represents the richness of our lives and experiences. It's all there, adding to the detail and color.

In food circles, people talk about layers of flavors and a flavor profile. Well, you don't get that from one ingredient; you get that from a balance of many. And God knows I'm not original in the sense that I created something new as a vocalist. The proportions and balance of those who inspired me are what created me.

In the lore of rock and roll, there are legendary, almost tragic-heroic figures who were said to be can't-miss talents but who never made it—people like the 1960s British singers Frankie Miller and Terry Reid. Terry was rumored to have been the first choice to front Led Zeppelin and later to have been offered the vocalist slot with Deep Purple. Instead, nobody's heard of him. Frankie Miller sounds like the blueprint for Rod Stewart. And sometimes I wonder: Could I have lived like Frankie Miller or Terry Reid? Could I have maintained the same passion if it hadn't led to commercial success along the way? Well, the truth is, I had no interest in not having commercial success.

I suppose everybody wants to be famous. But what are we doing to reach that goal?

Don't kid yourself, the bands that have done the best didn't fall into their success, and they certainly didn't sustain it by accident. Nobody who's around for decades stays there by chance. It's work, it's thinking things through, and regardless of what they say, it's a hunger and thirst to stay successful. If you don't have that from the start, you won't achieve success, and you certainly won't sustain it. You have to be clear about what you want and how to get it. Without a plan and a work ethic, you might as well say you want to fly.

What separated Robert Plant from Terry Reid? What separated Rod Stewart from Frankie Miller? Probably everything *other* than their talent. It's how hard they worked.

The playing field is not level. I don't think it is in any aspect of life. But opportunities are there for the person who works hardest. I'm not saying it's easy. I'm not saying it's fun. It's that much tougher for somebody with a facial difference or a physical disability. Even so, it's possible.

Is it fair? No. But if we let "fair" hold us back, then we become victims. And that's not acceptable. No matter how much we cry foul, only we will suffer in the end.

We can't win if we don't fight. We can't win if we don't play. So for me, at the worst times, it's always been about fighting to get through it.

I've never had a feeling of hopelessness. I've had feelings of despair, but I've never believed that any situation was permanent. We have to take control and acknowledge our pain and then move through it. Hope is based on shaping the future, not on seeing today as permanent. And that is the key to being able to dream big.

Of course, the future doesn't happen on its own. We make it happen. And hope is just acknowledging our own role, our own agency. The future is never set in stone, and for that reason alone, there is always hope.

I can't imagine giving up. It's so against my nature.

Because I really believe that we are the masters of our own destiny.

4

A FIGHTING OPTIMISM

ometimes people say to me, "I'm thinking of pursuing music."

And I say, "Don't."

If you have to *think* about it, you shouldn't do it. Do it only if you are *compelled* to do it.

I didn't really have a say in what I was going to do. I did it and do it because I *have* to. If you're considering a career in music, don't bother. You need to have a passion, an insatiable passion that you won't compromise.

There's a gap between feeling compelled to do something and making it happen, though, and the bridge is an empowered sense of hopefulness. Ultimately I have an outlook rooted in optimism—but a fighting optimism, not a passive optimism. An optimism of agency. An optimism that I have the power to make my life what I want it to be—as opposed to just wishing everything turns out okay on its own.

The difference between someone who wants to be something and someone who's actually going to accomplish it is also a sense of structure and a sense of steps—a process. It's not enough to want something. We can want it all we want, but if we don't have a sequence or a battle plan, it won't work.

Take my friend Chris Jericho. Chris was told he was too short to be a professional wrestler. But he decided to ignore the rules. He decided he would work harder than anybody else—and he made it.

The rules only stand until they're broken—and that is the essence of dreaming big.

I'll never have the foundation, background, or technique necessary to be a great chef, but that doesn't mean I shouldn't go forward. The idea that I paint or don't paint based on my knowledge of painting is self-defeating; whether I cook or not should also not be based on actually knowing what I'm doing. Again, that's self-defeating—after all, who knows anything when they first start? We can't get anywhere without taking that first step.

It's been said that the secret to getting ahead is getting started. Though that doesn't mean we can't ask questions when we need to.

I like stumbling around when I get started on something. Actually, that's kind of how I approached the guitar. I took a few lessons and then went off on my own. Later I tried another teacher, but I found that she didn't want me to go ahead of her lesson plans. So if I was supposed to practice one particular thing before a lesson but ended up working on additional stuff, that wasn't okay with her.

But that kind of approach just isn't in my nature. I like people to be there if I have questions, but don't tell me to slow down.

If we acknowledge, identify, and embrace who we are and what we are, then the potential is that much greater. I've painted entire pieces with a palette knife. In a sense, I wanted to tie one hand behind my back, not have the ability to add detail but rather to give the impression of things and then let the viewer's eye fill in the rest. I did that purposely to steer myself away from what I don't do well anyway. I'm not going to paint photorealistic pieces.

Identify who you are and what you are, and then embrace that rather than fight it in order to be something else.

If we define what we're *incapable* of, then we embrace what's possible. We eliminate the waste of going after what's futile or the things that don't represent who we are. By removing that waste, we embrace our full potential. It goes back to this: if I had decided to become a mathematician or a rocket scientist, I'd be broke. By eliminating the things that were out of the question, I gave myself that much more potential to do what was possible.

Of course, there were things I thought at one time were impossible for me, only to find later that my assessment had changed. For example, there was a time when I genuinely thought it would be impossible to be a good father, and yet I evolved.

Part of learning, part of exploration, is changing our horizons.

In the beginning, I just wanted to be happy. Simple, right? Well, that turned out to be pretty complex. And when I thought about being a parent, I knew I wanted to be a good parent, but I didn't believe I had the wherewithal. Both of those things came with time and work—and, in fact, informed each other. After all, how good a parent can we be if we don't know ourselves and aren't comfortable with who we are?

Those sorts of transformations don't happen overnight, but becoming a good parent and a fundamentally happy person have been perhaps the most rewarding accomplishments of my life. And they are also the sorts of transformations that led me to other possibilities: painting, theater, cooking, writing—whatever it is. I pursued becoming a famous musician with everything I had because, for one thing, I knew I was capable of it. When I saw the Beatles, I said to myself, "I can do that." Well, based on what? I couldn't play the guitar. I was deaf in one ear. And yet, without intellectualizing it, I innately knew: *I can do that.* The other thing pushing me along was that I was desperate to be happy. But I found out once I had achieved music stardom that I still wasn't happy— and that realization moved me ahead of where I'd been.

Accomplishing whatever we set out to do is the stepping stone to another level. It's another rung on the ladder. We never know where we're going to end up. We can only start, and once we start, every step we take, we can see a little more clearly ahead of us.

Of course, oftentimes we need a guide. We need somebody to show us options, show us techniques.

When it came to singing in *The Phantom of the Opera*— when I took over the lead in the production in Toronto in 1999—I saw the challenges. I had difficulty figuring out how to remedy certain things vocally, so I met with a few vocal coaches until I finally came across somebody who got it. He understood, and he said to me, "They hired you because of the way you sing. Don't change the way you sing." Which was a relief, because another coach I'd seen had foisted a completely new technique on me. His technique changed my tone dramatically, which was difficult with only two and a half weeks before I opened in the show. Thankfully, here was somebody who said, "They hired you because they like what you have. Let's just deal with the little issues. Let's not throw the baby out with the bathwater. Let's address what needs to be addressed."

Experts in various fields can tell when someone is eager to learn something, and maybe they take that as an appreciation of what they do. It's very inviting when somebody else is interested in what you do and wants to learn. I know it's always appealing to me. I helped a young man get into college a few years back. He wanted to pursue music, and his family asked if I could help. I sat down with him, and he played me a song to impress me. My role, I felt, was to be constructively critical—not to demean him or to discourage him, but to help him. After he got over the shock of my not being bowled over by his music—he said to me later that everybody always told him how great he was—he wanted more. That quality is hard to turn away from—when somebody looks to you as a mentor. It's not about my ego; it's more about paying it forward— and another way to live on in another generation. With this young man, I got to help somebody achieve what he wanted.

These kinds of situations aren't forgotten—by us or by the person we're helping. They are opportunities for us to share our knowledge with somebody else to help them achieve their goals, their dreams.

5

THE ONLY RULE
SHOULD BE:
NO RULES

We have a choice in life. We can choose whether to spend life saying "Why?" or to spend it saying "Why not?"

I've gotten the most out of life when I've said "Why not?"

Honestly, we can't know what's behind a door if we don't open it. Unless there are insurmountable, irreparable consequences, we have far more to gain than we have to lose by taking a crack at something.

Unlike some people, I'd rather fuck up than not try.

Thinking there are finite goals in life narrows our potential to take the ultimate journey, to take the ultimate trip. It limits us in what we're looking for or looking at. We don't get to absorb what's going on around us, which may affect where we ultimately want to go. The work we do to get where we think we want to go should get us where we *actually* go. Because life is fluid, and the goal we're pursuing shouldn't be finite. In the process, we may decide that where we've gone isn't where we want to be, so we decide to go elsewhere. We can't be too fixed in what we see as necessary accomplishments, because along our way we may find something more important, and if we have tunnel vision, it may blind us to our potential. Something that may appear to be a diversion could actually be the more rewarding path.

It's a problem when we set goals for ourselves that constrict us from changing course. The goal of KISS in 1973 was: find a manager. But if we had stuck to the well-trodden path, we'd never have found Bill Aucoin. And without Bill, who knows how things would have gone? Maybe a different manager would have tried to push us toward conventional decisions, and we never would have become the KISS that is recognized and loved forty-five years later.

When it came to realizing our dream as KISS, we broke every rule in the book. Most of what we've done is contrary to what would seem logical. When people say, "Why did you choose Peter or Ace?" or "Why did you choose to work with Gene?" the answer is surprisingly simple: because it felt right.

Honestly, nothing about the four of us would've necessarily put us all in the same band. If we had tried to put together a band of like-minded people, we would've ended up with different people in the band. There's no way we would've come together.

Once we joined forces and started to write songs and play out, it didn't seem strange to us to go with Bill Aucoin— who had no experience in management—as our manager. It was no more strange than wearing white makeup and making our own T-shirts. We knew exactly what we were doing. Going with the status quo or listening to people say "Be like us" is something I've never had any interest in—whether it was putting on the makeup, taking off the makeup, having a manager who had never managed, signing with a record company that had no real experience with a rock band— the list goes on. Just doing things the way that felt right, as opposed to the way that everybody else did them, seemed totally natural.

I'm glad that following the rules works for some people. But it doesn't work for me. Never has. And that's one of the keys to my success.

Why not?

Even though our manager had never managed anybody, he clearly understood the band. We were a band with white makeup and eight-inch heels. We weren't what was currently popular at that time—we weren't John Denver. There had never been a band like ours, so why shouldn't we try a manager who wasn't like existing managers? The normal way of doing things can give normal results. Extraordinary ways of doing things can give extraordinary results.

Of course, when you operate that way, you'll also make mistakes and face setbacks. But learning from mistakes fuels success. If you don't give up, a mistake is just another step toward success. If something doesn't work out—whether it's in the kitchen, in our professional lives, or in a relationship— it doesn't mean failure. It's just more fuel for success. After all, we can either repeat our mistakes or use them to plot a change in course.

I don't regret any of the departures KISS made as a band. They were essential. They had consequences, but it was never going to be the end of the story. I needed to do those things, and to deny them ultimately would have denied the band and myself. I needed to write "I Was Made for Loving You," for instance. I needed to.

The premise of KISS, when we got together, was "no rules and no boundaries." And that's what people embraced about us. So it would be contrary to suddenly say, "I'm going to live within another set of boundaries that the fans set." At the dawn of the 1980s, we started to experiment musically. I was willing to accept the consequences of what I did, but I also felt the fans had to understand that our premise of no rules and no boundaries was part of what they had accepted in the first place. As fans, they championed us because we did things our way. Thankfully, most of the time it also has been something they love. But I need the freedom not to feel handcuffed by their expectations.

Don't get me wrong. There were certainly troubles during the *Dynasty* era. Ace's alcoholism and drug use were out of control, so he was no longer reliable. Peter's drumming was substandard enough that the producer he had worked with on his solo album, whom we hired for *Dynasty*, didn't let Peter play on the album. Gene's focus was clearly on pursuing a career in Hollywood and left little room for making KISS his priority. I was more focused on serial dating and a never-ending shopping spree rather than writing the kinds of songs that celebrated a life I now saw only in the rearview mirror of my newly purchased Mercedes. The band was so splintered and dysfunctional that *Dynasty* was the result of all those components, good and bad.

But I wasn't manipulated, coerced, or strong-armed during the making of *Dynasty*, *Unmasked*, or *The Elder*. I made decisions based on my life at that point. I don't think they were the wrong decisions. They were necessary at that time. I needed to do "Shandi." We needed to make *The Elder*. After all, these decisions got me to where I am now.

Even so, in anything we do—me or anyone else—we have to be able to take a breath, step back, and ask, "Is this good?" Which is not the same as asking, "Does someone else think this is good?" I'm talking about a gut check, an honest assessment.

We lose the plot when we try to please other people instead of making it the priority to please ourselves.

And in the case of *The Elder*, it was a desperate attempt to seek validation from people who would never give KISS that validation. So at some point after that album, I felt almost like when I'm in a car and mindlessly driving, only to find myself wondering, "Where the fuck am I? When did I take the wrong turn? How did I get here?"

Perhaps *The Elder* proves that the most effective motivation has to come from within. When we do things to placate others, or for someone else's agenda, it's pretty hollow. If I'm going to fall on my ass, I'd rather do it while doing something

I feel compelled to do rather than while doing something someone else wants to do.

KISS was lost, and we had forgotten who we were and why we were. As we had with *Destroyer*, we looked to the producer Bob Ezrin to guide us, in part because he'd done a brilliant job on *Destroyer*. If he didn't exactly abandon ship during the making of *The Elder*, he certainly took a lot of shore leave—meaning we were without a captain a lot of the time. Much like with *Destroyer*, we were in uncharted waters during *The Elder*, but this time we had nobody to guide us.

We tried the best we could and were sincere, but we were deluded and tainted by our success. Our achievements didn't spur us on to be better at who we were and what we were doing. Our achievements gave us license to do less. Success gives everyone the opportunity either to sit back and get fat or to grab the next rung of the ladder, and that's where we failed.

We began to get complacent and lazy, and we lost the hunger. I'm not even sure "hunger" is a good word, because hunger implies that you need to be starving to have desire. Hunger shouldn't just come from starving; it should come from wanting more, wanting to raise the bar as opposed to sitting back and wallowing in your achievements.

If someone becomes successful, that literal hunger is gone, but creative hunger and hunger for ideals and standards should never be gone.

We were no longer in the first blush of success, and we had become complacent with success. I was dealing with having money to buy things, with security guys—and this changed the way I saw things for a while.

People may sometimes lose sight of all the complicated elements that contribute to a situation. KISS not only had fame and a certain new desire for validation from our peers; we also had a need for validation from our little sycophantic support groups. For so many reasons we found ourselves leaving behind the music that had been made by four hungry guys who had wanted to take over the world. In a sense, we felt we had accomplished that and didn't know what to do next.

None of us had any desire to make a hard rock album, or a heavy album. Ace might say he wanted to at that time, but that's like me saying I wanted to fly. We can't fly without wings. Ace was totally inebriated, so, yes, he may have wanted to make a hard rock album, but he wasn't capable of doing it.

We shrugged our shoulders and got excited with something that, in some ways, was easier for us to do: use a very familiar outline, used a hundred times before, and go in a different direction with it, because we didn't have the chops or the teeth to do what we needed to do. But, hey, even passive decisions are decisions. If you do nothing, you've still made a decision. Nobody should ever kid themselves. We took the path of least resistance, which is not that different from surrendering. It would have been more of a challenge to make a hard rock album. That would have taken a lot of effort.

At the end of the day, we were half-assing the work. I'm all for exploring different avenues, but it's important to do it from a position of strength and excitement, as opposed to being dazed. That's just wandering onto a path. It's just as easy to wander off a cliff.

That being said, everybody's vision was clouded, and what we did was misguided and of our own doing. For me to sing some pseudo-opera tune like "Odyssey" with a bogus Broadway voice reminds me of Alfalfa singing "I'm in the Mood for Love" in *The Little Rascals*. But anyway, it started from the wrong place. It started with the wrong reasons. There was no righting the ship.

Our choices flow from always having a reason why we do things. We question ourselves, question our foundations. Why are we doing this? Is this the right thing to do?

I guess one thing I can say in defense of *The Elder* is that we were not content merely to keep doing what we had already done. Nobody can re-create the past. The past is spontaneous and honest, whereas in any creative outlet, to try to re-create spontaneity is forced. It's the antithesis of where we came from, which was a place of innocence, and oftentimes creating by what we didn't know. Trying to fake that would have been impossible.

All the things that turned out to be problematic or distractions were the things that went along with success: enablers, people to open the doors. We wanted bigger, broader success, though in the end, we found out that all those things were detrimental to the success of KISS. But we had to attain the success to realize that. We had to do it all. We were compelled to do it. We needed to.

Besides, I couldn't have written "100,000 Years" at that point. I was still searching.

Fortunately, as my mom always used to say, "Nothing bad ever happens."

After all, *Creatures of the Night* couldn't have happened if it weren't for our no rules and no boundaries manifesto and an attempt to reclaim our identity—if not re-create who we had been, at least reconnect with the *reasons* we had been. *Creatures* was the pendulum swinging all the way in the other direction. That was change for all the right reasons. It was an amped-up, supercharged version of what KISS had done before.

It took those missteps and that state of complacency and creative gout leading to *The Elder* to get us back on the right road. I don't think I have ever wanted success and an outlet for my musical creativity any more desperately than when I saw it slipping away, when I saw complacency and the poisons of success breaking my connection with what had made me want to be successful in the first place. The past thirty-five years of KISS wouldn't have happened had we not teetered so close to the edge.

I have no regrets with KISS, none at all, because here I am, nearly fifty years later.

A lot of people say they have no regrets as a way of being bullheaded. When I hear people say it, I get the impression that what they're really saying is "I don't make mistakes," whereas I'm saying, "I make mistakes, but the mistakes are still valuable."

Mistakes got me here.

What's the saying?—"Communism is the longest and most painful route from capitalism to capitalism." In the same way, that malaise we felt—or whatever was going on—was necessary to get KISS from where we were to here. It was a long route back to home, but we had to experience it.

Why not?

6

OWN YOUR
ACTIONS,
OWN YOUR
OUTCOME

When I was younger, I had a lot of dos and don'ts, rules about what I required of myself and others. During my teens and early twenties, what I regarded as acceptable behavior from people around me was so strict, so stringent. But I found that these parameters weren't based on life experience. My standards were based on some crazy notions that, as a kid, I had set up in my mind, all rooted in my limited experience of the world beyond my home. The rules had all been established kind of arbitrarily.

Turns out we can't just conjure up those sorts of rules or parameters. We set ourselves up for misery or failure by expecting things of ourselves that aren't realistic or that are based on fantasy. We have to experience life before we know what is and isn't applicable and positive for us.

I made my life difficult and made having friends and socializing difficult by holding everybody to a standard—an inflexible, almost mechanical perfection—that no one could reach. Any mistake somebody made or anything that somebody did that annoyed me was reason for expulsion from my circle.

A girlfriend once said to me, "You're never going to be happy because you're too judgmental and expect too much from everybody." She was right. I wasn't happy. It's a bad idea to set up—even unknowingly—a situation where we're bound to fail. There's a difference between setting a high bar and setting an impossible goal. That goes for everyone.

One of the things I find interesting at this point in my life is to look back at times when I said things to friends and lovers and behaved in ways that, in hindsight, were appalling— but were very much in keeping with how my parents acted and spoke. It made it very difficult for some people to be around me, and it certainly affected some relationships.

My mom sometimes said to me or my dad or other people, "Who the hell do you think you are?" It's a horrible thing to say, but when I was young, I thought nothing of saying that too. If I was angry or somebody said something I didn't like or behaved in a way I didn't like . . . "Who the hell do you think you are?" It can be intimidating to hear something like that, and to make it worse, I said it like I was mad at the person.

I knew that saying this was demeaning and dismissive. But I said it anyway.

Another thing I remember saying in the course of arguments or conversation was "This discussion is over." And it worked sometimes. Though just as often the person would look at me and reply, "What are you, crazy? This discussion is *not* over."

I should've looked at myself in the mirror and asked, "Who the hell do you think *you* are?"

Part of the way I tried to establish a sense of security or safety was to hold people to my set standard, which was too rigid to be realistic. At the time, I felt there was safety in being able to decide boundaries, to decide how people could behave and what was acceptable and what wasn't. It gave me a sense of control over situations—though of course it was a false sense.

One of the earliest times I can remember being forced to examine my own behavior—my own shortcomings, really—was on a tour in 1979. A woman who was working backstage at the food service, where we could grab dinner, gave me an unexpected life lesson. I was with the band and some crew members, and we were teasing and making fun of some people as we ate. As this was going on, the woman became visibly upset. It was a strong emotional reaction: I would say she was truly aghast.

"It's okay," I assured her. "They don't mind. They like it."

I guess I was trying to dismiss the cruelty as part of the usual backstage antics.

"That's not what matters," she said. "You don't treat people the way they allow themselves to be treated. You treat people the way they *deserve* to be treated. You treat people with the respect *you* would expect."

Her words were like a sledgehammer to my head, and to this day I've never forgotten them. The way she put it was so articulate and concise that I immediately got it. Not that I had ever seen myself as cruel, but I immediately realized that this behavior I had deemed acceptable was in fact totally unacceptable. And it took somebody pointing that out to me, pointing out my behavior, to give me an aha moment. The sentiment was, of course, something I certainly knew was right, but I'd never given it sufficient thought in the context of my own behavior. Me, the kid who'd been bullied in the schoolyard, making fun of someone? What the fuck was I doing? I wouldn't want someone to do that to me, so why was I doing it to someone else? Once the woman voiced it in those words, I realized I had been wrong. It was valuable, constructive criticism.

In a similar vein, it's interesting to be able to look back and see that I wasn't so innocent in dealing with girlfriends, wives, bandmates—whoever it may have been.

On the 2017 KISS Kruise, I spent a little time with Peter Criss's ex-wife Lydia. We had a Q&A panel with Lydia; Michael James Jackson, who produced *Creatures of the Night* and *Lick It Up* and helped us get back on track in the 1980s; and our first security guy, Big John Harte. It was terrific, and people asked great questions. I hadn't seen Lydia in a long, long time. When she was married to Peter, we had a contentious or uncomfortable relationship at times, though certainly in hindsight it wasn't one-sided. On the Kruise, it would've been easy to avoid contact with her because of experiences decades ago. But it also would've been a missed opportunity. I had, after all, played a part in those strained relationships.

I hoped that she wasn't the same person she was back then, and I know I'm not, so the idea of seeing somebody in a new light was intriguing. In the end, I wanted to see her—and it was indeed great to see her. It was rewarding and opened up far more avenues than living in the past would have. It's always great to have a chance to celebrate with somebody where we are today, rather than steep ourselves in the discord of where we once were. There's a coming together and a celebration of where the road has taken us.

I almost wonder what I had been fighting about with people like Lydia. Sometimes we tend to get into the rhythm of doing something a certain way. To see her again and instead give her a hug and introduce her to my family was awesome—and I think we both felt that way.

That was also very much what I hoped for when the KISS reunion happened with the founding band members in 1996. The idea, at least for me, was to take advantage of how we had grown individually so we could correct some of the mistakes and go forward. That hope turned out to be very short-lived. But I see a great potential for reward in revisiting old situations and old friends or people from our past after we have a new perspective. It can put to rest any doubts we have and allow us to reflect on what caused the problems in the first place. With closure, it's possible to remedy, rectify, and move on; it allows us to move on without the what-ifs—and I don't want what-ifs in my life.

How I had seen Peter and Ace when they left the band was based not only on my perspective back then but also on how I had affected them with my own behavior. So I thought it was worth taking a shot at healing. Not to take advantage of that possibility—if only to resolve a lot of questions—would have been a shame. Though some people didn't see the opportunity the same way. At the beginning of the tour, it felt like a new beginning, but that feeling didn't stick around.

Of course, in the case of a band, any reunion is complicated by musical factors too. When Peter came back into KISS, he was born again: he was a born-again KISS-tian. He was joyous in knowing that he was back, and he seemed cognizant of the mistakes he had made. At the onset, he said that he would never make the same mistakes again. So his musical shortcomings wouldn't have been insurmountable if he had continued to be willing to work on his playing— which he was when he first came back. He was very open to adjustments. I don't want to say "criticisms," but let's call them "helpful directions." This was something he'd never been able to handle in the past.

Unfortunately, things with Peter changed dramatically almost overnight.

Back in the 1970s, Bob Ezrin, who produced *Destroyer*, had gotten Peter to play things that should've been impossible for him. But Peter pulled them off. It goes back to the fact that we know how much something is worth to us by how hard we're willing to work for it—and once the reunion got under way, Peter wasn't willing to work to improve his playing. It descended into a destructive situation. I remember thinking, *If you're John Bonham and you're a prick, that's one thing. . . . If, on the other hand, you can barely play* and *you're a jerk, then what's the point?*

Of course, at the end of the day, the only person I can change is me.

In a band, for it to work, everybody has to do their job and contribute what's necessary to make it work. When someone doesn't do that, I can't do it for them. I can't do it for them any more than I can make up for what the other person in any kind of failed relationship isn't doing.

With Peter, ultimately it wasn't about his not being able to play; it was about *why* he wasn't able to play. It was about him as a person—his failure to commit to being the best he could be, his lack of wanting to do the work. That is much more the point.

And to some extent, the same was true of Ace. Again, the same resentments that plagued the early days of the band resurfaced, and those resentments came from internal factors. I just became the target, the personification of whatever those guys were dealing with on a personal level.

Throughout the reunion, Peter felt that the room service people treated him disrespectfully. He went right back to finger pointing and blaming everyone else. You'd think most hotels hired their staff based on their ability to be disrespectful to Peter Criss, because he found such people in every hotel in the world. What could we do about that? I believe that if we all had been committed to bettering ourselves as musicians and working as a team—if we all had understood our place on the team and worked individually to be better at what we did—maybe we could've continued.

When Ace and Peter were out of the band, the remaining members had taken the band down to the dirt and built it back up. So there was no way Ace and Peter were going to return and have everything as it once was. Plus, during those years—the non-makeup years—I had learned a lot of aspects of the business and touring that I hadn't known before. So for Ace and Peter to come back and be considered equals was ridiculous. It was so unfortunate when they became more concerned with how much money I made versus how much they made. A whole lot of people in the world are richer than I am, but it doesn't eat at me at all.

It was sad. But I don't cry about it.

Still, it was terrific to get back together, because it put to bed any doubts or thoughts I'd had about possibilities. Without the reunion I would've had to live with those thoughts. But I've been sleeping real soundly since then, I can assure you.

I'll drag something as far as I can, but at some point I know there's no point in dragging it any farther. When is it enough? When it's enough. It's just that simple.

I got to a point where I was confident that the band wasn't failing because of me. I'd pushed it in a different direction, and since it was still failing despite my efforts to be different, then it wasn't due to me. I was certainly cognizant of what the band had dealt with before—my shortcomings and inflexibility, my insecurities and defenses—but by 1996, fifteen to twenty years later, I was a different person.

From the beginning, the original thinking behind KISS was that the four of us didn't have to do an equal amount of the work; we each just had to give 100 percent of what we were capable of. That might not be the same thing within any given song. And certainly not within the band as a whole. We weren't all the same when it came to how much we each contributed creatively to the music or to the overall image or staging. But for us to share equally, we had to contribute as much as each of us was capable of contributing.

And once again, those guys were not doing that.

But, again, does anything bad ever happen?

I don't think so.

We dealt with crisis management as time went on. I'm sure that Ace and Peter at this point are either baffled by or dismissive of how we have evolved and what Gene and I have reached in our lives, but the irony is that without the two of them there would be no today. Even so, they had to realize that what's true today isn't necessarily true tomorrow—being in a band isn't a birthright.

When KISS started out, we believed it was all for one and one for all, and that was the way it would remain until the end. Well, that's fine until you don't believe it anymore. Then what do you do? Do you take your ball and glove and go home? That's for each person to decide. I was in a band with three other guys who shared a sense of camaraderie and commitment to this force called KISS. Like a lot of things in life, I assumed that was forever. Marriage is often the same way.

What happens when forever comes to an end?

I refuse to let anyone else decide my fate. I refuse to let anyone else decide my life experience, because we get only one shot at this. I refuse to let a bad bandmate shut down a good band. I refuse to let a bad marriage negate the potential for a good one. I refuse to let a bad marriage make me cynical about the ideals of a great marriage.

Each person has to make their own rules to live by and, as I've said, seek to revise and improve those rules on the basis of their experience.

If someone doesn't want to play within the rules, then find someone else to play with. I was stunned when a therapist said to me once, "If you're working really hard in a relationship, you're in the wrong relationship."

I was like, "What? It's that simple?"

Yep.

And I don't think family gets a free pass. The fact that you share common blood with somebody shouldn't allow that person to taint, compromise, or detract from your life. This is the only life I will have, as far as I know, so I don't care whether it's a sibling, a mother, a father, or another relative—bringing something in that pollutes or dilutes my experience or the experience of people I care about is unacceptable.

If you have to work at a relationship too much, you're in the wrong relationship—no matter what. We all make things much more complex than they need to be sometimes. As opposed to the complicated and unrealistic rules I tried to impose when I was younger, this is something incredibly simple and totally based in common sense and reality.

PART TWO

RELATIONSHIPS AND FAMILY

7

LIVE FOR OTHERS AND LIVE FOREVER

These days, because my frame of mind is different, I'm able to think about the positive things I took from my childhood—maybe in an effort to understand in as much detail as possible how I can best support my own kids. I also think that when we go through the process of deprogramming or unlearning, we can look at the past in a new way, and the negative aspects of it don't maintain the same hold over us that they used to.

I remember my mom would scratch my back when I was little, and nothing felt better than that. She had a way of scratching my back that nobody else could replicate. She also used to rock me to sleep sometimes, and I loved being on her lap. I identify very much with some of my mom's food too. When I make meatloaf for my kids, I always say to them: "You know who made great meatloaf? Omie."

It's interesting to realize the conflicting ways my mom has lived on in my life.

Again, my parents may have trampled on their kids a bit, but I don't think it was ever consciously intended to hurt. It was what they'd experienced growing up—the ideology that you don't make your kids feel too comfortable or too complimented or give them too much approval because withholding all of that will toughen them up. And I laugh, because I know the best way to toughen kids up is to make them feel secure.

There was always an awkward disconnect between my parents and me. Even so, they were very much about being there for me. It may have been inconsistent and erratic because of their histories, but unlike a lot of parents, they always said, even when I was an adult, "You can call us at any hour."

That was not the case with many people I knew. Their parents would tell them not to call after ten p.m. My parents? I remember calling them in the middle of the night. Despite whatever they lacked, they were there for me in the best ways they could be. And that's important. When I split up with somebody in my early thirties and was pretty broken up, my mom came into the city to see me. It was an odd juxtaposition: despite their shortcomings, my parents were always concerned for me. When I was going through my divorce in the late 1990s, I called my mom and sobbed on the phone.

So I have to say that despite all the odd or unhealthy aspects of our relationship, my parents were there in ways a lot of parents are not. I certainly often focus on their deficiencies, but they both had another side that was very committed and devoted. And that is the side I wish to emulate—I hope without the rest.

This comes back around to the idea that we never die, because who we are lives on, for better or worse, in our children and their children. Who we are, and who we become, has consequences. How we live matters, because it's what we pass on to our children and those around us—and it's what out-lives us.

My mom's spirit lives on in what I carry of her. I can't make meatloaf without thinking of her. I can't eat it without thinking of her. I made it during one of my dad's recent visits, and it was clear to him what it meant. So, yeah, I carry the good and the bad. The bad I've come to terms with, and the good I embrace fondly.

I certainly hold memories dear that keep my mom alive for me. Still, though I don't quite understand it, I don't find myself missing her. Before she died, I was afraid of her pass-ing away, and then it turned out differently than I'd expected. Her death was huge the day it happened, of course—it was life changing. We are always our parents' children. But ever since she's been gone, I haven't missed her. Physically she's not here, but whatever I got from her is. So for some reason the only void I feel is that I don't get to see her, but that's the only thing that's changed. What I experienced with her is all still here.

When my dad's gone, it will be much tougher—because I still have a connection to my parents through him. The more profound loss is when both parents are gone, because then we're orphans; no matter how old we are, we're then children without parents. Once my dad's gone, I fear I'll become what we all really are inside: a kid. And at that moment, we are children who have been abandoned, for lack of a better word. That eventuality is something I wrestle with.

I'm well aware with all my children, at their various stages of development in life, that I'm an integral part of who they are and who they will become, and I embrace my role. There's comfort in knowing that my path to immortality will be paved by helping my children find their own road. It's hard for people to think of the world without them or of no longer existing. Most religion as it's written and articulated is just a way for people to come to grips with the finality of life. I don't have a problem with that, because in my mind, people continue to exist. Stories of an afterlife may help people in their struggle with the idea of the world without them. But guess what? The world existed before we were here, and it will continue without us. We leave our mark, and at least for me, that provides a sufficient sense of comfort.

There's consolation in knowing that we continue. Though that didn't come into play for me until I had children. Until then, I used to wonder what life was about. What was the point? Well, now I know the point is what we do in our lives and what we leave behind. That is very calming and has put a lot of my questions to rest.

So, in the same way, my mom and dad continue on through a meatloaf recipe or memories of my back being scratched or going to a museum. They are both still with me.

And because of how involved I am with my children—and I see it already with Evan because he's older—I know I'll be there that much more.

We get out of something what we put into it. And what we put into our children is paramount to who they become and how much of us continues in them. In that way, we are linked. They know it and we know it. Evan and I are very close because of things we've gone through and spoken about and shared. That started at an early age. And I already see instances of this in Colin, Sarah, and Emily as well, in the questions they ask and in how Erin and I respond. They are all a continuation of our input, our influence, our spirit. That's really what this is all about: our spirit lives on in those around us, in the people we affect the most.

Obviously, for me, children are a part of that equation. But we live on, too, through interactions with nonfamily members, through things we do for others. We can never do too much good, and each time we do good, there are two beneficiaries: the person we help and ourselves. Yeah, I know it sounds corny. If somebody said this to me twenty or thirty years ago, I would've thought it was dopey. But perhaps as we move farther down the conveyor belt, we can start to figure out what the endgame is. And it really is true that helping other people achieve their goals or helping them through their struggles means they carry us with them. When we do something good for someone else, they remember it.

The greatest thing I did in life was to stop being judgmental—stop judging and stop being intolerant or unsympathetic. Once I let go of those things, the world looked better. It looked less ominous, and it looked less menacing and ugly. Doing something like that adds a whole existential aspect to the concept of taking pride in what we do and doing things for the sake of our own personal edification. There's a kind of cosmic scope to it as well. Because it's not all for nothing. That's what I used to believe, and a lot of people probably also believe—that it's all for nothing.

What's the point?

Well, it turns out the point is that we can make our mark, a mark that will keep us present beyond the time we're here on Earth. It's impossible for us to live forever, but our spirit can, through what we impart to the people around us.

8

LIFE BECOMES WORTHWHILE WHEN WE MAKE OTHERS FEEL WORTHWHILE

They say that the two most important days in our lives are the day we're born and the day we find out why. And that's a great insight.

Except there's no single day that we find out why. Life tells us why in an ongoing way. Experiencing life and taking it all in is a continuous process.

Certainly, having children was a major defining moment in my life because it made clear to me that being a parent—being a good parent, being a father—might be the most important reason I was born. Though parenting, too, is a process that evolves. Just as we never arrive in life, we never arrive as parents either, and our dreams and goals shift as a result of circumstances and experience.

Throughout the course of being a parent I've had the sense of its importance reaffirmed. If we are consciously aware of our actions, we will constantly fortify, reevaluate, and acknowledge our purpose. Over time, various ways I have either protected or steered my children, and continue to do so, are added to the answer to the question of why I'm here.

Even the idea of being a parent changes. Some people think that being a parent is about being "present" and providing for their children—but how do we define that? No one has to be a parent to feed someone, for example, so that can't be the root of it.

I was talking to my daughter Sarah recently, and I suddenly said, "I can't believe I'm your father." I've said this to her before—I say it to all my kids. What I mean is that I'm so blessed to have been able to reach this point.

When we set goals related to how we want to succeed in life, we never understand the full scope of life's possibilities. We can only imagine what we can comprehend. The joy of being a parent and seeing these people who are part me is mind-blowing.

There's an incredible primal component to being a parent, and part of the power I feel is from something that is not a conscious decision. It transcends that. It is the essence of religion and spirituality. The ultimate affirmation of life is birth. Although I can't articulate it, what's so stunning is to suddenly understand the meaning of life and how life is perpetuated, and how, in essence, we never really die.

We are the remnants of our parents, and we continue on through our children.

This realization was so enormous in scope to me that, again, it opened a door to something I didn't even know existed: the potential to give a child everything I didn't have, and also to heal myself by doing it. There is a reciprocal joy.

I've made the conscious decision that the best way to lead is by example. I become a better person when I make sure I'm not only honest with myself but also honest with my children. I ask myself, *Is this behavior I could explain to my children?* Thinking this way eliminates many moral dilemmas. It's a simple gut check. Even if I didn't have kids, I could apply the same thinking in a more general way: *Is this behavior I could honestly defend to future generations?*

A tobacco company once offered KISS sponsorship and much needed financial compensation at a time when we were trying to rebuild the band during personnel changes and upheaval, and our money was dwindling. But if we had accepted that money, how could I explain that to my children? We passed. At a later point someone was interested in partnering with me to create a coffee-table book of porn stars, and I thought about it. No matter how I window-dressed it, it again kept coming back to one thing: How could I explain this to my children? Well, I couldn't, so it was another no.

In the case of porn specifically, people have to decide for themselves whether or not it works for them. But for me, the book would have been legitimizing something I wasn't comfortable with, and I would have been doing it because money was involved. I want my children to know that money can't change my values. If I'm hoping they will emulate what I say, they should also be able to see that I back it up with what I do. What we do inspires people much more than what we say. That didn't resonate with me until I got older, but now it's my mantra with raising kids: lead by example. It's not what I say; it's what I do. Or as I heard another parent say, "I'm watching your feet, not your mouth."

Sometimes people look at couples who don't have children and think, "Oh, isn't that sad?" Well, who's to say? Nobody is automatically a good parent. We don't automatically give our children what's best for them—even if, as it was with my parents, we have that intention. Not everyone automatically puts their children before themselves—some people are too selfish to do so. I certainly don't think that just by having a child we necessarily develop those desires or drives.

My childhood led me to look for ways to validate myself because I didn't get sufficient validation at home. Now, as a father, I think it's important to tell my children I'm proud of them when they succeed at something. But it's also important—very important—to say to them, "How does it make *you* feel?" That is, to put them in touch with their own feelings so they're not dependent on *my* approval as much as their own. As Colin and Sarah have already shown themselves to be terrific students, with test scores and grades I certainly never had, my saying "Boy, that is really terrific" has led to "How does it make you feel? Does it feel good to do such a good job?"

I want all my children to realize that doing well makes *them* feel good, as opposed to just making me proud. I want to stress the internal rewards of doing a good job, not just the external praise. Positive reinforcement is great, but equally important is to teach children that success feels inherently good. Accomplishments should make them feel good, and it's not as necessary for them to get the approval of someone else as it is for them to feel their own approval.

I regard this as extremely important with my children. It's important to me that I tell them this because I didn't hear it when I was a child. But again, it's also important to say "How do you feel?" That connects the dots for them.

It makes my dad feel good, but I feel really good too.

I have always wanted to give my children something wonderful, to help them appreciate the things I appreciate. Validation comes in so many forms. Recently Colin was gazing out our bedroom window and said to me, "Dad, look at that beautiful sunset." I knew that we, as his parents, were making that crucial difference: I must be doing something right if my children see the beauty in the world around them that other people miss. That's life affirming to me. That means I'm going to leave something behind that's better than who I am.

A couple of years ago I was telling someone that my adult son, Evan, was very grounded, very socially conscious, very cognizant of his obligations to the world and to society. Then I added, "All things I was clueless about at his age." Evan is so far beyond who I was in my early twenties. At nine, Sarah has compassion and empathy for others that is deeply touching, and it is the result of her processing what she has seen at home and embracing it in her own way. Emily, at seven years old, has a grasp of social interactions and a confidence that makes her one of the funniest and most joyous children I've ever seen. The fact that others agree, and that she is mine, only deepens the profoundness. These qualities had no bearing in my life when I was younger, but all this is the ultimate reward, the ultimate measure of my own life. I'm doing something right, and that's life affirming.

Look, everybody thinks their children are special. When other people tell you your children are special, there's something rewarding about that. Those accolades mean a lot to me. I love it when somebody comes over to my family in a restaurant and says, "You're a great dad." Well, I know that, but it's also nice to have it recognized.

As I said before, I don't believe trying to be a great parent is universal. I've seen a mom look at her child—who couldn't have been more than five years old—and say, "You make me sick." So, no, I don't give that credit to everybody. Having a child doesn't automatically make anyone a great parent. For me, parenting has to do with giving my children what I craved and wanted so desperately when I was young. Not material things, but a sense of worth, a sense of joy in the world, a sense of no judgment—all things I wasn't given. I have an opportunity to shape my children in a way I wasn't, and to reap the rewards of doing that. Because I believe we heal ourselves when we do good for others.

When it comes to living on in another generation, I'm happy that the things I've been able to learn, independent of my parents, are now getting passed down. I'm breaking the cycle. It's not necessarily analogous, but a child who has been abused has two choices: to become an abuser or to be the opposite. I know what I saw. I know how I was treated. I am determined to take a different road with my kids.

Sometimes I'm stunned by what I see out there. I'm stunned when parents still put themselves, in one way or another, before their kids. I can't fathom that. I see people who say they put their children first, but then they qualify it. Don't qualify it. Put your children first.

I want to be the best parent I can for my kids. I expect that from myself. When my younger son, Colin, says to me, "You're the best dad in the world," I say, "That means a lot to me. I try." Mind you, most kids will say their parents are the best in the world, but I want my son to know I work at it. I *try*. I *want* to be the best parent. I want him to know that it's not something I take lightly.

That's different from a lot of other people. And the rewards are so much greater. It removes a lot of the chance in how children will turn out, because the children are being guided and fueled by their parents. Yes, children will be who they are and each one will be different, but children start life as a blank slate and we parents are the ones who do the initial writing on it. We give our children the values they start out with—and we can save them a lot of trouble if those values are worthwhile.

We're not going to change our children's personalities or their aspirations, but we clearly give them their code of honor, their ethics, their morality. We can spell that out to them, or they can see it in action. I want to make sure my children see it in action.

One thing that's particularly important to impart to children is the difference between tolerance and acceptance. Because I want to help my kids be nonjudgmental and empathetic. I know there's been a sort of movement built around the idea of tolerance, but I'm not interested in tolerance. Tolerance isn't what's called for; acceptance is. Embracing. We tolerate pain. We tolerate sadness. But that's not the same as willingly accepting something. Acceptance is a choice we make.

Tolerance is a good legal standard so people can't discriminate. But I want something on a more personal level. It's a bit like the difference between what is lawful and what is ethical. People can stay on the right side of the law, can stand up and say, "I didn't break the law," but then do some horrifically unethical things. I'm not interested in teaching my kids to tolerate differences in other people. I want to teach them to accept and embrace those differences.

Anyone can quote from the Bible; and you can find anything you want there, from brutality to kindness. But anybody who uses the Bible as grounds for either hatred or intolerance, or tolerance with the belief that someone is going to hell, doesn't make the world a better place. I've found in my life that by being kind and accepting—and understanding how difficult life can be for others and how we all deserve to be loved and happy—makes life so much better. To give that to my children early in their lives, as opposed to letting them stumble through life the way I did, is a gift to them and to me. To carry around hatred or intolerance or judgment is ugly.

The bottom line is, who are we to judge other people? Who are we, for instance, to decide or to pass judgment on who anyone can love? We're blessed to find love. If my kids see somebody who's different from the norm, I make sure to tell them to imagine how difficult that person's life is, how brave that person has to be. If we see a homeless person on the street, I remind my kids that that person was also once a child in school who dreamed of being president or a star.

I want to break everything down to its most human form.

I want all my children to know it's okay to feel pain, it's okay to hurt, it's okay to cry. I've done all that. Only weak people don't. Strong people do. I'm real clear on my job. When baby birds leave the nest, they have to be ready and they have to have knowledge. We should set them up to be able not only to handle life but also to embrace it. Not to go out there and battle. It shouldn't be a battle out there. We should give our kids the tools to go out and enjoy life, to be suitably educated to deal with whatever they need to deal with and believe that they can.

It's what we owe them.

And if we don't do that, they'll suffer for it.

I've always found that I'm most effective in conversations with people when I just relate what I've done. Maybe that information will enlighten them. Maybe it will give them some glimmer of how to apply the same things to their own lives. But I'm not in any position to tell anybody how to live—including my children. When Evan reached an age when I thought we needed to talk about drugs, I didn't say to him, "Don't do drugs," although I certainly believe that. I thought the most effective way to talk to him was to let him know in more practical terms what doing drugs can lead to: "Remember so-and-so? He's dead. Remember so-and-so? He's broke."

Basically: Here's the lay of the land. Here are the tools. Now you decide.

I continue to follow this same approach in many different forms, and the results are resoundingly evident in who my children are, how they see the world, and how the world sees them.

9

THE BOUNDARIES WE INHERIT LIMIT THE DISTANCE WE CAN TRAVEL

Nobody loves to acquiesce in a relationship just for the sake of keeping the peace—that creates a powder keg. Over time it just builds resentment—whether it's within a marriage, a friendship, or a professional partnership. I'm not saying anything new. But you have to decide what's important; you can't just go along with something for the sake of keeping the peace. It will eat at you—and what does it say to the other person about you? Who are you, and what are you willing to stand up for?

It might be more unpleasant, but you can't fix a decayed tooth without a root canal.

I can assure you that forty years ago, my current scenario—a marriage grounded in mutual respect, with compromises based on embracing each other, dealing with real issues, and letting go of minor grievances (like the correct way to put on a toilet paper roll)—would have been as impossible to me as learning Greek. But it comes down to what we are preprogrammed to do and what ultimately works in life for each of us.

The core of the problems in my first marriage was that we each fought to get our way—because of what *not* getting our way represented to each of us. There was so much baggage that anything we argued about or disagreed over was often just a symptom of a power struggle. We could struggle over picking fabric for a chair or choosing a color to paint a wall. But I realize now that wasn't the issue. The issue was control—who was in charge and who got their way—which would have been much more productive to address head-on. Deciding on the color of a wall had very little to do with the color and everything to do with whose will was going to be imposed on the other. That's what we all need to strive to avoid: giving something misplaced value or misplaced importance instead of dealing with true issues, and letting problems manifest in things we can't fix. In other words, on the surface a conflict may appear to be what kind of furniture to have in the house, when really what's at stake is who's in charge.

KISS experienced similar problems. At times in the early days there was resentment about who was at the front of the stage or who had the most songs on an album And rather than deal with that, we tried to undermine or outvote each other. Peter, for instance, used to throw drumsticks at me when we were onstage. If he could have, he would have rigged the stage with land mines. He had a sort of exclusionary zone in front of the drum riser, and if I drifted into it during a show, he pelted me with sticks—instead of dealing with whatever frustration he had in his life. Or with the resentment he felt toward me for being younger and not having gone through what he had gone through to get where he was. Or with the fact that the songs were mine, or that I was doing the talking. Whatever it was. Passive aggression is just misplaced anger. Maybe if he had dealt with it, he wouldn't have needed to act like that.

Of course, in the band, we all had that to an extent. There were times when I was very clearly annoyed at Gene, and rather than address it, I did things that alienated him, alienated me. My anger may have been directed at the things he did—giving undue credit to himself, getting more interviews, or getting more photos—but the way I dealt with it was to be a dick.

We all would do better by addressing the real crux of whatever issue we have. In various relationships earlier in my life, whether personal or professional, I often didn't or couldn't address the crux of a problem. I don't mean to suggest that any issue is one-sided. In hindsight, I see more than I did in those moments. It always takes two. Nobody is guiltless.

In the context of marriage, one aspect in particular is a microcosm of how I go about things today: interfaith marriage. Erin is Catholic; I'm Jewish. It was critical that we talk that out ahead of time instead of being faced with the issue later in our relationship. Because the biggest impact of not hashing it out wouldn't have been on us; it would have been on our children.

In interfaith marriages, from what I've been told, the most common issue is that kids assume that they don't belong in either religion. In other words, unless it's agreed upon and discussed ahead of time—what the course of action will be and how the children will be raised and how each parent will or won't participate—it sets children up not to know what to do. So are you going to bring up your child as a Buddhist? Great! Are you going to bring up your child in a Protestant sect? Fantastic! Jewish? Terrific! But if that's not the case, then what exactly are you going to do?

In my case, because of my upbringing, I had inherited the idea—based on what I had seen in my parents and relatives—that my children had to be raised Jewish and only Jewish. But over the years I found that what I owe myself and my children is perhaps different from what I was *told* I owed myself and my children, or what my family or relatives expected. So in my case, even if it sounds odd, we tell our children they're 100 percent Jewish and 100 percent Catholic.

Nobody wants to be a fraction.

But my children understand the diversity within the family. We celebrate Christmas and Easter, and I go to church to celebrate some important Catholic holidays. Not because I'm Catholic but because my wife is. It's clear to my children that I'm Jewish, and quite honestly I grew up in a household where the idea of going into a church was suffocating. But by embracing my wife's heritage and background, I embrace my children. There's room for autonomy while embracing your partner's background.

Going to church is another concrete way to demonstrate empathy to my kids. I tell my children that the only religion to steer away from—and that I want no part of—is one that presents itself as better than another. Or as right. I try to make sure my children know that religion is based on faith, not fact; faith is powerful, but nobody should dismiss another person's faith because they think their own is somehow more rooted in factual reality.

I feel an obligation to Jews throughout history and the people I grew up around who had concentration camp numbers tattooed on their arms; I have a responsibility to teach my children about the Holocaust and about the plight of Jews. What they decide to follow in terms of a theology will be up to them. But being kind, accepting, loving, and charitable has to take precedence.

Of course, for kids it's perfectly normal to equate their favorite holidays with the ones when they get gifts. And if we were going to make a quick synopsis of all Jewish holidays, we would just say, "They tried to kill us, they didn't, let's eat." Gifts aren't the focus. But of course my kids also love Hanukkah, and I try to make them aware that it's not a poor man's Christmas. Every year before we light the candles I have them tell me the story of Hanukkah and what it means, and the stories of Antiochus and Judas Maccabeus and the oil that lasted for eight days instead of only one. I want them to have a sense of these stories and also the idea that there were and are people who want to stop religious freedom, and that's never okay. Sarah and Emily like to wear kippahs, so why would I say no? This is a celebration of inclusion, and Erin is with us and we all sing together and light the candles and play with the dreidels. When Evan is away from home, he lights candles on his own—so it resonates with him and has stuck.

I'm well aware that we don't have Rabbi Man or any kind of cool iconic figure like Santa, so in terms of competing, we're in a deficit there. Hanukkah is quaint next to Christmas. Between Erin's parents and brothers and sisters, the number of presents my kids get at Christmas is enough to open a store. And that's part of their celebration, something that Erin brings to our kids' childhood and experience. But we don't divvy up the gifts. They're two different holidays and two different experiences, and part of two different religions. So they're not in competition, because that would turn it all into something unpleasant, uncomfortable, and stressful. Competition by nature is not relaxing. Having two holidays from two different religions competing against each other is contrary to the way celebration is supposed to be. But if you're strictly talking gifts, Christmas wins! Hands down. And I'm okay with that.

We have to figure out what really matters to us individually and what we're okay with, and that entirely changes life. Experiences are so much more fun when we're not threatened by something or turning it into something it doesn't need to be.

So, yes, you can have both.

Regardless of whether it may seem contradictory, my children were baptized. I would like all my children to have a bar or bat mitzvah too. Could I ever have imagined my children being baptized with holy water? No, but I have to say those were amazing, beautiful, rich moments. Baptism is part of who they are, part of who the woman I'm spending my life with is, and part of who I am now. Erin and I decided that neither one of us should bring up our children without acknowledging our own heritage—it's important they experience both. Ultimately they will make up their own minds, and honestly, whatever they choose is fine with me because they will be well-rounded, loving children and adults who will contribute to society in many ways.

Being at Evan's bar mitzvah was joyous; so is having an Easter egg hunt or going to Christmas Mass with the family. Again, that's who we are. We are all of those things.

Before we go to bed every night we say prayers. Some nights the kids pray to the Father, Son, and Holy Ghost, and some nights they don't. But no matter what they pray, they acknowledge God, and they have the sense that nobody can know what is right or wrong; we can only acknowledge and celebrate our lives.

If religion teaches kindness and charity and understanding and acceptance, then it's good.

For religion to survive, it must change and reflect the times; religions should be living, breathing things. Knowing right from wrong, treating people the way we ourselves want to be treated, doing good because that's what God wants—those are timeless ideas. I know Catholics who don't adhere perfectly to the dictates of their faith—they practice birth control, for instance—and I believe that for a religion to work it has to be realistic and applicable to our lives. Now some might say the opposite—that one's life has to conform to religion. But I don't agree. For instance, some sects of Judaism say that children are Jewish only if the mother is Jewish. Well, I say bullshit. I'm Jewish, and if I'm Jewish, then my child is Jewish. Whether or not everyone agrees with that is irrelevant. When you embrace who you are with pride and without excuse, you dignify who you are.

The way Erin and I deal with religion is just one key to the success of our relationship: if something bothers or annoys one of us, we want it out in the open. Otherwise, things snowball, and at some point we don't even remember how the avalanche started. The way to keep that from happening is to address it before anything accumulates. If something bothers you, let the other person know how you feel. That way, maybe you don't need the root canal, because the rot never sets in. It's preventive dentistry.

People go to therapy because decay has set in. Maybe in a lot of instances in relationships we can avoid that decay by brushing after every meal, by flossing—by addressing things before they give way to rot.

Of course, sometimes we may come up against situations where the other person doesn't want to do that. Then we have to make a decision. Because we can't change other people. There's no point in spending time thinking, "If only they would do this" or "Why are they doing that?" At some point it boils down to, "Why am *I* allowing this? Why am *I* going along with this? Why am *I* here?"

That's what we all have to come to terms with. Why are we here? Is it beneficial to be here? What are we getting out of it? When somebody won't acknowledge or address something, then the rest is up to us. The way something affects us has more to do with ourselves than with the other person. The way somebody's behavior affects us is all about us. We are the ones who decide how it affects us and what we do. Either we find a way to make a relationship work for us, or we leave. But we don't try to change the other person. We can only change how we take in and respond to their behavior.

Listen, I'm not Gandhi, but I bear no animosity toward people who have wronged me or misled me or been dishonest with me. They're just gone. They're no longer a part of my life. It's part of the imperfection of life and how we deal with it.

When we've been hurt, we're often motivated by vengeance, by getting back at somebody. But the thing is, when we're happy, we don't need to make anyone else miserable.

We don't want to replicate what somebody did to us. We realize at some point when we're happy that creating misery never creates happiness, especially through revenge. Never. Revenge is ugly. It only puts us in an ugly place doing something ugly.

10

STRIVE TO RAISE THE BAR, NOT TO LOWER IT

When I got divorced from my first wife in the early 2000s, I felt an overwhelming sense of failure. I had certainly never imagined getting divorced—probably because my parents never divorced, despite their unhappiness.

How do we define love? We are tempted to define it on the basis of what we saw at home. And the turmoil I saw growing up was in some ways mirrored or replicated in my first marriage. It almost seemed the norm. Even though I thought I was going in the opposite direction from my parents, I ended up walking into similar dynamics—into uncertainty, lack of support, tension, all the things that I'd faced when I was a kid. And somehow I thought I could make it work because I could make everything work. Well, I couldn't. The only person I had control over was me, and my control just meant that I endured the marriage. My first wife and I were just the wrong people at the wrong time.

Even so, the idea of divorce was terrifying. But when a relationship isn't good, it has to end.

It's too easy to blame the other person, just like it's too easy and completely absurd when people say they're not lucky in love. The first thing we have to do is accept responsibility. When children are involved, it's important for all parties to agree that the children won't become collateral damage, that they won't become pawns, and that they won't be used as a threat. For some reason, some people have a lot of difficulty agreeing on that.

As for why my marriage failed, the fact that I chose who I chose was a clear sign that I had a lot to figure out. The nature of our relationships is a great indication of where we are in our lives. Who we choose is a pretty good mirror of our state of mind. Hence, sixteen wonderful years with Erin, and the only uncertainty is what great things lie ahead.

As I've said before, we all must realize that the only person we can change is ourselves. Knowing this allows us to be much more powerful, because we use our true powers as opposed to imagined ones. All my missteps led me to the clarity I had when I met Erin, proving that my true strength comes from being able to change myself and not waste effort on trying to change others. The fact that my prior relationships didn't work shows that I was confused and still believed that I had the power to make things the way I wanted them to be. And because I felt I had that power—I had, after all, achieved all my professional dreams—I hadn't yet learned that I didn't have the power to make other people do what I wanted them to do.

In the wake of my divorce, trying to protect Evan quickly became my priority. I chose to spend virtually all the time when he was with me one-on-one, just the two of us—to protect him, to calm him, and to let him know that I was there 100 percent. Bringing another woman into our circle, let alone our house, would have been an assault on his security, and more confusing and more of a threat than anything he needed to deal with.

Of course, the lines of communication need to stay open between separated couples. We must be able to voice concern over parenting methods or actions that we may find questionable or detrimental—though children should never be confronted with whatever fighting goes on. Who's right and wrong should take a back seat to what's best for the children, and one thing that's for sure best for any child is for the parents not to bad-mouth each other. That should be forbidden—for the sake of the child.

It's baffling to me that people are willing to hurt their children by saying bad things about their children's other parent or by not being supportive. I certainly had disagreements with my ex after the divorce, just as we had disagreements when we were together, but we were determined to make this process as safe and comfortable for Evan as possible and acknowledge how difficult and awful this was for us and for him. We assured him that we would get through it and that no one was to blame.

It boggles my mind when I see people criticizing their ex in front of their children. On top of the insensitivity, anyone who does that is denigrating a child's parent. It's frightening, it's confusing, and it potentially puts the child in the horrible position of having to take sides. During a divorce, the last thing that should happen is an innocent child being put in the line of fire or used as a tool or a pawn. In the very worst-case scenario—and mine fortunately was not that—it comes down to this: Do you hate your ex more than you love your child? It's that simple. Stop with the rhetoric, stop with all the machinations, and which is the stronger feeling? Your love and desire to protect your child, or your ill feelings toward your ex?

If estranged parents can put aside the acrimony and hostility for the sake of their child, I highly recommend their seeing a therapist. Not because it's court ordered or because they have to, but because they should respect their partner's concerns; and perhaps bringing in a qualified intermediary will allow them to pick a course of action that is in the best interests of their child, even if they may not necessarily agree with it.

Involving therapists or going to counseling is not a move of desperation or weakness. It can be productive and constructive. You put aside the fact that you're not together and not getting along, and you concern yourselves solely with the best way to handle this process for your child. You want to protect your child, and if your biggest concern is truly that child, then seeking an outside voice can be a great help. It shouldn't be a tool used to punish an ex. Again, do you love your child more than you dislike your ex? It's always important to take the high road—if for no other reason than to demonstrate empathy to your children. You don't need to point anything else out in terms of your parenting versus someone else's, because when your kids get older, they'll figure it out on their own. To put poison in their ears or to speak poorly about their other parent is counterproductive, because the child loves both parents.

I can't pass judgment on parents who remove themselves from their child's life or poison or pollute their life because of a divorce or separation, but I can say that's not what being a parent is in my mind. When my children suffer, I want to protect them. When my children are scared, I want to soothe them. When my children are sad, I want to either cheer them up or listen to them. I want to validate my children. Many times, that's all they need: to be heard. A child should not end up being collateral damage.

When we break the foundation under our children by saying that Mommy and Daddy are no longer going to be together, that is inconceivable to them. From the day they were born, Mom and Dad had been not only their foundation but their world. Yet now that's going to break. I saw with Evan how terrifying and incomprehensible this process was to him. My role had to be to protect him, to be there for him, and to get him through it.

There's a lesson to be learned—that things can be terrible but we can get through them. Not easily, and not without pain, and not without acknowledging the pain. But we can get through them.

Evan is the poster child for divorce. He's done great. He can't imagine his mom and dad being together, and in his own way he figured out the dynamics between us and why we're not together. When he's had graduations or other milestones, we've celebrated as a family unit and, when appropriate, with Erin and his brother and sisters. And make no mistake, Erin—without ever posing a threat to the relationship between me and Evan—became a key factor in his seeing the dynamics of a healthy relationship and how we all can come through the worst upheavals to a better place than where we started.

This was another case of our experiences defining who we are. It was so clear to me what my childhood lacked, and I was determined—despite divorce or anything else—to provide that for my children. We all can realize and reaffirm in countless ways what our lives are about and what our active participation should be.

ABOVE, LEFT:

**MY YOUNG DAD AND
A CHUBBY LITTLE
STARCHILD.**

ABOVE, RIGHT:

**MY PARENTS ON
THEIR WEDDING DAY,
SEPTEMBER 24, 1948.**

LEFT:

**TWELVE YEARS OLD.
I WISH I COULD GO BACK
AND GIVE HIM A HUG.**

NEW YORK CITY TAXI and LIMOUSINE COMMISSION
TAXICAB DRIVER'S LICENSE
EXPIRES MAY 31, 1974

STANLEY B.
EISEN

1 8 1 4 4 2

YOU MUST RENEW THIS LICENSE BETWEEN MAR 5 1974 AND MAR 15 1974

NEW YORK CITY
TAXI and LIMOUSINE COMMISSION
87 BEAVER ST. – NEW YORK 10005 N.Y.
MICHAEL J. LAZAR, Chairman.

30M/12/71

LOVE HER ALL I CAN

I remember the times I was lonely without her
Now she's mine and I spend my time dreaming about her

[CHORUS]
Love her all I can and try and understand
The things that make her glad the things that make her sad
I'm a lucky guy I hardly ever try
and when the world looks bad she's never never sad

She's so easy to please and it doesn't take money
We can have a good time when the skies aren't sunny
Repeat chorus, 1st verse, and chorus

BLACK DIAMOND

Out on the streets for a living
The pictures only begun
Living in sorrow and madness
They got you under their thumb
Ooh Black Diamond, ooh Black Diamond
Darkness will fall on the city
It seems to fall on you too
And tho' you don't ask for pity
There's nothing that you can do
Ooh Black Diamond, ooh Black Diamond

LEFT, AND BELOW:

TWO FORTY-FIVE-YEAR-OLD, NEVER-BEFORE-SEEN SHOTS OF A NEW BAND CALLED KISS.

BELOW:

STUDIO 54. WATCHING IT ALL HAPPEN WITH ANDY WARHOL, ANNIE LENNOX, AND FRANK ZAPPA. A GOLDEN AGE OF EXCESS.

RIGHT:

1975. ALL GLARE AND HAIR.

PHOTO: BARRY LEVINE

ABOVE:

WORKING OUT TODAY. YOU CAN'T WIN AT ANYTHING YOU DON'T START.

PHOTO: BRIAN LOWE

LEFT:

AT HOME. MY HAT, MY GUITAR, AND MY PAUL STANLEY PUMA SUEDES. STYLIN'!

LEFT:

BACK TO 531 WEST 211 STREET. A BOY LEFT, BUT A MAN RETURNED.

BELOW:

A MAGIC MOMENT WITH SARAH, EMILY, AND COLIN.

ABOVE:

ROAD WARRIORS READY FOR THE END OF THE ROAD.

PHOTO: BRIAN LOWE

BELOW:

SOUL STATION. SEAN, GAVYN, CRYSTAL, LAURHAN, AND RAFAEL. PART OF THE TRIBE, PREACHING ONSTAGE AND LOVING LIFE.

I WENT FORWARD WITHOUT REALLY KNOWING MY DESTINATION.
BUT I KNEW WHEN I GOT THERE, IT WAS HOME.

PHOTO: BRIAN LOWE

11

UNDERSTAND THE WHY AND STRUGGLE LESS WITH THE WHY NOT

In one form or another, we're all addicts. We just pick our poison. Sex, drugs, and rock 'n' roll? Those options are all still available. While I never thought the drugs were part of the equation, the other two went hand in hand. As life moves on, though, changes and choices need to be made. Rock 'n' roll remains. But for me, marriage and monogamy also go hand in hand. So I made a choice, and that was to be with Erin and only Erin.

To live with our choices and not struggle with them over time, we have to be clear on why we made them.

My decisions have to be rational, well thought out, and based on how a change will affect me. In committing to be faithful to Erin, I considered not only how it would affect my life if it came out that I betrayed that commitment to her, but also the personal burden of carrying that dishonesty even if she never found out.

Somebody once asked me about monogamy, and I said that it's something people have to decide for themselves. But part of that choice is what I just said about living with knowing that I've been dishonest. Someone else would be privy to the secret other than me. And if someone else is privy to something, then no doubt other people will be as well, because there are no secrets. If I don't want people to know about my doing something, I don't do it, because most things get out. And even if it didn't get out, I would torture myself about it. For me, there's no room for dishonesty in my relationship. Women are still as beautiful as ever, probably as available as ever, but I will take a pass.

If we see somebody who's appealing or attractive and enticing on any level, it's important to think, *Wait a minute. I have X amount of years with my partner and can depend on that person to continue to build something together.* Why would we gamble on what's behind Door Number One when we've already won the grand prize?

At this point in my life, it's clear to me that what I have is a gift. I will not jeopardize that gift for a momentary situation. I weigh what I have versus what I had in the past, and as much fun as it was back then, none of it had the depth or held the rewards that my life now gives me. Somebody once said to me, "I'm married, I'm not dead." That applies. But to make things work, we have to make conscious decisions and know the value of what we have. Not knowing why we're doing something makes it much harder to understand its value. Craving or attraction will always be there, but if I gave in to it, I would lose more than I would gain. It's certainly important to feel attractive too, but knowing you're attractive to the person you truly love and admire should always make you feel like the best-looking person in the room. For so much of my life, attraction led without any hesitation to sex. That was the natural rhythm of things—no pun intended. It was just the natural flow of events. But that has changed. One no longer leads to the other.

It's great to be able to proudly show people photos of my family and know this is what I have.

So for me, the struggle isn't so much of a struggle, because I tend to be very pragmatic. And weighing the pluses and minuses, it's a no-brainer. That may not negate the attraction on some level, but it makes the idea of following through on that attraction out of the question. Certain women probably think I'm either stupid or gay. Actually I'm neither, but I'm definitely happy.

Now I acknowledge the attraction and someone desiring me, but it doesn't go beyond that. Though again, I understand why. Otherwise, it would be much harder to say no—in fact, there would be no reason not to follow through. We need to be clear on why we're doing or not doing something. If we don't know why we're not accepting advances or proposals, then maybe we should just go ahead.

Every choice in life is much easier to make when we know why we're making it, but that's lost on a lot of people. Decisions become easier when we understand the pros and cons and the consequences of doing one thing or another. So, to be honest, I don't find it difficult to say no, despite sometimes being faced with some real interesting opportunities. But would I like myself if I said yes? No.

On all different levels, in all different situations, we have to know the reasoning behind our decisions. I don't ever want to reach a point in my life when I have regrets about what I didn't do. And yet there are plenty of things I haven't done. The key is that I know *why* I didn't do them. And thus I know why the decision is not regrettable.

When any of my relationships has been in trouble, it's always been important to me to know why it was in trouble. And if and when it came to an end, it was important to me to know how I participated in it falling apart. In previous relationships, there were moments when I considered getting involved with somebody else and I thought, *No, I have to end this first*. Because I wanted to be clear about why that relationship wasn't working, and I didn't want it to be because I had been dishonest or had cheated.

By the same token, these days I always tell Erin when we run into women I know—in all different senses—from my past. It's important that nobody ever has a secret with me that she's not privy to. She certainly knows my past. I'm a big believer that the fewer secrets we have, the freer we are. That's pretty much always been the way I approach things, but particularly with Erin, the idea of not acknowledging that somebody in the room is somebody I've known or that somebody she's talking to is somebody I've been involved with is far more uncomfortable for me than telling her. Likewise, Erin is beautiful, outgoing, and extremely bright, so for me to believe that her life began the day we met would make me an idiot.

I never thought life would end up like this, but it makes sense. I never knew things would be like this because I had to take the steps to get here, and each step made it more possible. I couldn't have fathomed the calm and satisfaction I have because that's not who I was. We learn as we go. We have to know what we don't want and understand what we were wrong about before we can know what we do want. I'm blessed because I have been able to find out what I was wrong about.

The mistake I made in many previous relationships was that I went into them looking for approval more than anything else. I looked for somebody who would pump me up and boost me. And that's not grounds for a relationship—especially when I often didn't even get the approval I had been looking for.

I can argue that I had not yet realized that ceding some control is part of having a relationship. In the case of my first marriage, that was in part because it coincided exactly with the time when I was forced to do the opposite inside the band—I had to consolidate control in the band for the sake of its survival.

But a relationship's success still comes down to who we're having that relationship with. We can't marry somebody who is at best ambivalent about giving up independence—the whole purpose of marriage is to combine. When we pick somebody who on some level doesn't want to do that and pulls away, the natural reaction may be to try to pull them closer, which makes them pull away farther, which in turn makes you want to try again to pull them closer. Pretty? No. Pretty futile? Yes.

A relationship should bring out the best in both people and not provoke the worst. Too often, we have an agenda in a relationship. And if things don't go the way we anticipate, we rationalize and find a way, because we have our agenda and we have our script. A lot of people think, "Oh, it'll work out when we're married" or "It'll work out when we have a child." Well, I'm here to tell you, it's not going to.

A good partnership or relationship can only be built over time. And it can only be built over time because it's dependent on how each partner responds to various situations, including critical situations, and on how they respond to each other's needs. Obviously the commitment has to be reciprocal, but our partner must be somebody we can depend on—and the extent to which we can depend on them in various situations can be determined only through experience. Anyone can be a good person when things are going well, but a person's real character is revealed when the chips are down.

I had a medical scare years ago, and because it was a very frightening prognosis at that moment, I called two women

I knew—one being Erin, whom I'd recently met. The first woman said to me, "Oh, that's terrible." And Erin said to me, "Where are you right now?" And that is what you're looking for: the person who drops everything to support you.

Erin and I dated for more than four years before we got married—and it wasn't because I wasn't crazy about her right from the start. But I think we both had to reach a point where we couldn't imagine not being together. That's way different from that first blush—which is awesome and can possibly be the first stone of a foundation, but by no means is an instant attraction to someone anything more than a fabulous psychological and biochemical reaction. I had years to see how Erin dealt not only with me but with her friends, emotional issues, medical crises, family problems. That's key to a relationship— seeing how the person we're willing to empower deals with things. Not surprisingly, Erin has never, ever disappointed me and has always been able to be there for me without any fear that it implies any weakness on her part. Security in ourselves allows us to do things without giving up our self-worth or self-respect. I've seen both sides of that coin in my own life and development—I had to deprogram my past, and experience the sense of self-assurance that came with that process, before I was capable of being there for other people.

I also love the fact that my wife blows me away with her intelligence. I am so thankful when Erin does or says something that makes me think, *Wow, I never would have thought of that*. It's a great thing. In fact, I'm suspicious of people who seek out "lesser" partners, people who want to feel superior by being with someone they regard as less intelligent or less together. That has to do with discomfort with oneself. I want to surround myself with people who are on the same path that I am on.

We always have to look at somebody's track record before we met them, because chances are that will dictate their future behavior. If your accountant has been sent to the slammer for fraud, there's a pretty good chance he's going to steal from you too. The only way to justify getting into business with someone who's been convicted of fraud—a situation I've faced—is to pretend the person will act differently toward you. But no matter who you deal with, it's never going to be you and them against the world. It's always going to be them against the world. You're never excluded from the treatment they've shown other people. Sometimes you may think you're joining a movement when that's simply not the case. If somebody has been ruthless or unethical with others, their same rules will apply to you too.

I learned at some point not to be surprised if I got screwed—in the less-than-ideal way—by somebody I clearly saw screw somebody else before. Earlier in my life, I was involved at various times with women who were cheating on their boyfriends or husbands. Time and again I just took it as the price of admission. Time and again the same brick fell on my head. But then I realized that being shocked at that behavior made me a fool. If I chose certain playmates—no pun intended—I shouldn't be surprised if they hit me on the head with a brick.

It's fine to go into a relationship with our eyes and our ears open. Love is sometimes blind. But it shouldn't be deaf.

When we get into a relationship—romantic or otherwise—with somebody who displays some kind of negative behavior, we may make the mistake of thinking that we're excluded from that behavior. Sooner or later, the way we see that person treat other people is the way they will treat us. If we choose not to see that, we shouldn't be surprised down the road. We're not excluded; we're next. That's who that person is.

Sometimes people say they want unconditional love. Well, the person who wants unconditional love is ultimately the person who's going to bring the least to the table. It's not about their partner. It's about what that person wants. Unconditional love means that they expect their partner to tolerate whatever they do, often with no regard for the other person. That's not a two-way street—and that's not love, as far as I'm concerned, which is by nature a two-way street.

I knew a woman who was recently separated from her husband and got steeped in asking why her estranged husband was saying this and why he was doing that, and I just said to her, "The real question is, why are you there? You can't change him. The only person you have control over is you."

The idea is: Rather than trying to decipher your partner's behavior, how about figuring out *your* behavior? Why are you where you are? Why did you choose this person? And why did you accept his or her behavior?

It shouldn't feel demoralizing to find out your relationship isn't as you expected. It's a chance to make a change—for the better.

PART THREE

SELF, HEALTH, AND HAPPINESS

12

KICK THE
BUCKET LIST

've always seen life as a conveyor belt. When we're young, everyone's ahead of us. As we get older, we start to see that the line behind us is longer than the line in front of us. It's sobering. But that's not a bad thing, because the reality is, we all reach our demise, and it makes the time we have here that much more precious.

For much of my life, I aspired to become more at peace with myself and more comfortable with myself and to become a better performer, better singer, better writer. At an early age, dreaming about being a good father was not in the cards. We can realize things like that only when they're close enough to see and feel. There are also times when we have to accept what we won't be able to do, and that's important. There's peace in being pragmatic enough to look at life and say, "Well, these are things I would love to do or do again, but other things are more of a priority for me at this moment in life."

We tend to look too far into the future when we're not equipped to have an answer. There is no ultimate goal or destination, because whether or not we reach our goal, the journey there fills us with new possibilities. We can only define ourselves today, and part of the joy of life is knowing that we will define ourselves differently in the future. That's the excitement of self-discovery.

Life is long, and in the grand scheme of things, anything we accomplish is just an opportunity to accomplish something else—something more, something better. It doesn't mean that any given accomplishment isn't important. It just means that it's of a certain moment. It's what we did today. But what will we do *tomorrow*? If we are truly motivated and if we truly value ourselves and see the potential in our lives, that thirst is never quenched. That hunger is never filled. Because it's not just a need; it's what makes life valuable.

At this point in my life, all of the amazing creative outlets I have make me feel good. I'd like to say they make me feel young, but that wouldn't be accurate—because I didn't have them when I was young. I had to get older to have access to them and the ability to see them. Painting, theater, writing books, my musical side project Soul Station. I find happiness in much more mundane outlets too, like simply being a dad or cooking up a delicious family dinner.

One of the keys to all of this: I kicked the bucket list.

We often make a fundamental mistake when talking about a bucket list: a bucket list should always be expanding based on our experiences, not getting shorter. If we're slowly checking off items on our list without adding new items, we're doing it wrong. You could say I have only one item on my bucket list: never to reach the end of my bucket list.

Because achieving something on our bucket list should open our eyes to something else we need to do. I don't think we should ever end up with everything checked off our list, regardless of how content we are with what we've accomplished. I achieved all I originally set out to do—I attained fame and fortune as the rock star I'd always dreamed of becoming. But in my case, that was far from the end of the story—thank goodness!

I've realized that I'm just as happy about discovering new items for my bucket list as I am about checking one off. In fact, that's the real excitement in life. The excitement is in discovery. And we can have the same sense of awe and joy in discovery as an adult that we had as children. In fact, the excitement is more pronounced for me now, in my sixties, than it was when I was younger, when I was too rigid in my thinking. If you're missing that, then you're not living your life fully. If your day is filled with the expected, then you need to open the curtains.

I started off by thinking life had a limited scope. It's easy to picture life like a TV screen and believe it's a certain size. Then experience shows us that it's actually the size of a movie screen, and then, hopefully, it reveals itself as the size of an IMAX screen. Life should be a series of panels opening to make our world bigger, because what we let into our lives and how we perceive and experience it defines who we are. And I should emphasize, who we are for *ourselves*.

I'm much more aware of who I am today. I'm as aware today of who I am as I was clueless about who I was in earlier years. As the picture grows bigger, we have to step farther back to be able to see the complexity of who we are.

Of course, it's still worthwhile focusing on specific goals. To try another metaphor, we can think of goals as tiles. We want to add tiles, sure, but we don't want to just stack them up. We want to lay them out and use them to create a mosaic that can represent the richness of our life. We need to make sure that these tiles assemble into something larger—the complete picture of our life. As we create this mosaic, it should necessitate our stepping farther and farther back to see the whole picture, to see its enormous size and the intricacy of it. At that point, we should also see the potential to fill in more: self-discovery should lead to more self-discovery.

Nothing brings me more contentment than knowing who I am and knowing that I'm more than I thought I could be.

I'll tell you something else: as with much art—and certainly with rock and roll music—even the imperfections are part of it. There's no such thing as mistakes. Tunnel vision is fine in our quest to accomplish something, but we should always be aware that any given accomplishment is not the end. It's part of this much larger picture.

Not only does this kind of approach—having a broader vision of ourselves and the world—make us more interesting at, say, a party, but it can contribute to the back and forth between all the various pursuits we engage in: we raise everything we do by raising anything we do. Not to mention, we're more engaging in our own heads. We like *ourselves* more. We enjoy *ourselves* more when we like who we are, and liking who we are is based on liking what we do and—especially—how we do it.

13

CHOOSING YOUR BATTLES MEANS YOU WIN MORE OFTEN

Most of us will face situations in relationships or in our professional lives that have the potential to immobilize us. We have to fight that with all we have. There's nothing wrong with licking our wounds, but once we've done that, we have to get up. Because—as we've all seen—when we stop moving our bodies, they become less cooperative. So get out of bed. Put on some clothes. And if at all possible, get moving. It may feel like we're carrying the world on our shoulders, but ultimately the only way to lighten that load is to move forward. Otherwise, we're crushed by it.

Among the lowest moments for me professionally were during the tour for *Creatures of the Night*, when we played to half-empty and sometimes nearly empty arenas. It was a horrible time. It's mind-boggling to think now that I could fall asleep backstage in the dressing room—but I was so depressed that I just could not stay awake.

It seemed there was only one possible outcome: the band was going to go down, and it was over.

But if I'd had a hopeful approach, I could've thought of all kinds of other outcomes—and things we could do instead of accepting that one outcome. Sure, I was miserable. But it didn't mean the band was over. It meant I had to fight to bring it back. Even if I didn't know what I was going to do, I realized I could and would do something. I had to fight to leave that feeling and situation behind.

I simply told myself: *This is not the end. This is not the final outcome.*

I was determined not to allow the ship to sink. One reason to keep going was to avoid giving the people who didn't like us the satisfaction of watching our demise; another was my refusal to let anybody except me determine the outcome of the situation. Funny how in situations like that, some bands will go onstage and give a half-assed show. Which makes no sense to me, because then you're penalizing the people who showed up. Don't be angry at the people who actually came. Give them something that they can go home and tell other people about.

If the band wanted to continue, the solution obviously wasn't to have fewer people next time. We needed to attract more people instead. So lashing out at the people who were there would have been crazy. What we needed to do was blow them away.

I spent a lot of time wondering what else we could do to change the outcome.

Taking the makeup off was one thing. *Creatures* was a terrific album and a great declaration of our resolve to come back even stronger. But it fell on deaf ears because people were tired of seeing us the way we had always looked. Maybe they were unable to embrace other personalities or other faces in makeup. And it was clear to me that people were listening with their eyes. I had wanted to take the makeup off for *Creatures*, but we didn't. So for *Lick It Up* it was a no-brainer.

After all, they say insanity is doing the same thing and expecting a different result. Well, if we had put out another great album with makeup on, we'd have been idiots. How could we take this to the next level? By making another good album and changing how we looked. You know, retaining the part that people still embraced and accepted and getting rid of the part that wasn't working.

When *Lick It Up* came out, it did well immediately, and we suddenly found ourselves being embraced, even by some of the critics, which was so strange to me—because I consider *Lick It Up* a good album, but *Creatures of the Night* is a great album. Others apparently saw it differently—and I would say that reaction is not coincidental to the fact that one of the album covers had us in makeup and the other didn't.

There was also an underlying motivation for me to want the band to take off the makeup. There's really no denying that with makeup, Gene is the face of KISS. But I've always been in essence the voice of KISS. Well, another way for me to get my due, or to get more of what I thought I deserved, was to take off the makeup. Because I was basically the same person I was with the makeup, whereas Gene relied on the makeup. In a sense, we changed the face of the band. And in doing so, I got to be recognized not only creatively and musically but on the street, which I also craved and enjoyed. I wanted that acknowledgment, which had been missing.

It had always seemed odd to me that when I read something in the media about KISS, it described Gene as the "front man of the band." It was always about Gene. But I thought, *What do you mean by front man? The guy who talks the most offstage? What about the guy who does all the talking onstage?* So now I was the lead singer. Indisputably the face of the band.

It served the band's purpose, and it also served my purpose.

Whether it was "Lick It Up" or "Heaven's on Fire" or any of the songs from that era, the band had a new dynamic—and a new focus. And if you look at the *Smashes, Thrashes & Hits* album, one person is in the center and bigger than the others. Which was appropriate. And, yeah, I enjoyed that. Plus, there was a feeling that went back to the code of the original band: as far as I was concerned, we didn't have to do the same amount of work, but we each had to give 100 percent. And when someone wasn't giving 100 percent, then I didn't expect them to get equal exposure or equal billing. If you want to be in the front, then you've got to hold up your end of the bargain.

Even at the most frustrating times, I never contemplated KISS breaking up. Too much worth, sacrifice, and commitment had gone into it. I'd worked too hard to get KISS where it was to throw it away. As far as I was concerned, everybody and anybody could leave; I was staying. I never pondered even taking a break. When a band takes a break, there's always a risk of never being able to get going again. I'd rather keep moving, even if the pace was slower or I took a few wrong turns. We risked losing all our momentum if we stopped.

I also had seen enough people who had left bands or dissolved them, thinking they could continue on their own. That's a tough awakening. For me to suddenly take off the makeup and go solo back then? I could've done it, I guess, but I don't know what the outcome would've been. KISS was an anomaly, so I don't know if the rules that apply to other bands also apply to us.

Then there was the name KISS—talk about brand recognition. Companies spend decades and millions of dollars to build that kind of respect and awareness. Other companies buy names that have been established. We established KISS as a band, but it became as recognizable as a brand, and to give that up would have been stupid. Even if I couldn't match the success we'd already had, it was a huge advantage to have that name.

But mostly, I liked the support of a band. I liked the security. I liked having other people to lean on rather than going it alone. That's why I got together with Gene in the first place—because I didn't feel I could do what I wanted to do on my own. I'd always wanted a band. I wanted team members. And that was as true ten years later as it was when I started out.

Often the best way to achieve goals is to assemble a great team; sometimes we just don't have that luxury. By the 1980s, the team around me was a frequently shifting cast of characters, and Gene was mostly absent. But there was one constant: me. That was okay, because it meant I was steering the ship. There's a sense of security in having faith in the captain, and I had faith and always have had faith in myself. As people came and went during those years, as other members' commitment waxed and waned, it boiled down to this: *How do I maximize what I have, and how do I make the most of the people who* are *here?*

Certain things I could control, and others I couldn't. Certainly, with the non-makeup period that balance shifted. I couldn't make guitar players do what I necessarily wanted them to do, so they either were asked to leave or they quit. I couldn't stop Gene from wanting to build a movie career, so I took up the slack. Ultimately, I learned not to depend on anyone else. And that has not changed since then, despite the later periods of stability within the band. It's safer and it's more effective. It's always risky to empower somebody else. We have to have trust in somebody, and that trust has to come through experience. It's not about a gut feeling. I don't give that trust to anyone except over time, after I see how they deal with issues, how consistent they are, how they deal with crises.

As far as dealing with the band in the 1980s, I basically took on sole leadership of it, I made the most of what I had, and I didn't dwell on what I didn't have. I wanted to do what I was capable of doing rather than get hung up in thinking about things beyond my control.

When I look back at those years, I see it was a pivotal time for the band, but there have been many—and it's always been about problem-solving. It's all about maintaining the freedom to keep pursuing our dreams, in whatever form those dreams have taken at a given point in the trajectory of our lives.

The band will always be my baby, and for many people—as well as for me, for much of the history of the band—that means not giving it up. Of course, my view on that, too, has evolved over time—not necessarily the baby part, but my willingness to give up my role in it.

I sent out a tweet last year with a picture of the Eagles in their current incarnation, without cofounder Glenn Frey. I wrote, "The Eagles tour has already added more shows due to demand. Seeing a photo of the band now with one original member is a testament to the timeless power and endurance of great songs, created over decades by musicians united in pursuing a musical vision and standard."

Then I started getting all these bitter responses along the lines of: "They're not the Eagles. These guys should hang it up. They're a cover band."

I was reading all this stuff, and then came another line of thinking: "Oh, Paul, you're saying that because of KISS. You're a cover band too."

I rarely respond to stuff like that, but this time I did.

> To the whiners,
>
> The hundreds of thousands who will love seeing the Eagles on this tour don't care about you, and will have a great time while you whine about which and what band isn't meeting your criteria. In a world where someone else is happy, your unhappiness doesn't matter.

And if you don't think I'm laying the groundwork for leaving the band, I have a bridge to sell you. I love the idea that the Eagles now is being led by a son of one of the founders (Deacon Frey), a founder (Don Henley), and a bunch of other guys. Or take the band Yes. There's not an original member in Yes. Yet do I consider them a cover band? No, because a band that exists over decades evolves through personnel changes and health crises. So do I consider this to be Yes? Absolutely. It didn't change overnight. Members have come and gone. The Eagles are the same way: Timothy Schmit is great, but he certainly wasn't in the original band, nor was Joe Walsh. And Deacon Frey was baby batter. Do I like the idea that the endurance of a band isn't limited to a particular set of members? You bet.

It's all about seeing your role, and I know mine: to give people the support and license to serve as their own advocate. Self-empowerment is the key to everything that I won by fighting against those who told me how things had to be or what they expected.

Understandably, someone may want you to fight. All I want to do is take that off someone's shoulders. You choose your fight. We all choose our fight. When we're at the biggest moment of our life, at its end, we need to make that decision with a clear conscience, knowing the decision is ours and ours alone. It puts so much in perspective for me; I've seen people leave this Earth who wanted to connect with somebody they clearly do not regard as a stranger.

My life is on my terms. At times when KISS looked like it was going to implode, and critics or the people who didn't like us were salivating, I would revive and resuscitate it in its death throes if for no other reason than the fact that nobody is going to tell me when it's over. That's not acceptable. I believe the band must continue, even if someone else might say the opposite.

I certainly know people who have said, "My band had to end because I'm not going to be in it anymore." Well, I disagree. Our band should continue because what we've created and what I've worked so hard for is still valid, and as corny as it might seem, KISS may function as a beacon of light for some people—it's so much more than the best goddamn show out there. It's the rising up of the underdog to win. Success has never taken that away from us. For that reason alone, I'd like to think it should endure. If all it means is *If I can do it, you can do it*, that is a message that will never grow old. I want to champion every person out there facing adversity.

The power and meaning of KISS can also transcend the individuals in it.

Some friends and people I'm close to have said to me that I must continue. They make it very clear that they don't want to lose their emotional connection to the band, its stabilizing effect on their lives. And I say, "I understand, but I did this in the first place to write my own rules—and that includes being able to say when it ends for me."

It's interesting, though, because the other side of the coin is people saying that some star athlete or other should hang it up because they're not as good as they were in their heyday. To that, I say, "It's your right to stop seeing them, but they owe you nothing. They've given you everything."

Nobody has to apologize for doing what they love. They get to decide if and when it's over for them.

And if it's over for you, you have the right to stop going to the games or listening to the music—whatever it is. You have the right to stop buying tickets. It's an odd idea that the people who have made you happy now need to go away because they're not living up to your expectations.

This has never been about anybody else's expectations but mine.

14

WHEN YOU FIND THE TRUE MEANING IN WHAT YOU'VE ACCOMPLISHED, YOU'LL FALL IN LOVE ALL OVER AGAIN

would say without hesitation that the most fucked-up people are entertainers. They crave attention. They crave approval and validation of their worth that they don't inherently feel, and they don't look to fill that void just through relationships; they seek it from a crowd.

For most people, the larger a crowd, the more intimidated they feel. For plenty of folks, being forced to stand in front of 20,000 people would be their worst nightmare. But I happen to know a lot of people who consider that their Disneyland. Because the people who are most insecure, if they have the wherewithal and the tools, use that platform to put themselves in front of mass adulation.

It's so apparent to me.

Why do bands want to be on tour all of the time? Because that's where they feel most omnipotent. That's where they feel most important.

Do they feel important when they go to the grocery store? I guess not. Do they feel important when they take their kids to school? Apparently the answer is no. The people who seek attention are the ones who are the most . . . I don't want to say maladjusted, but they have issues with self-confidence and self-worth, and they look for validation externally that they don't get either from the people around them or internally.

When KISS started out, people like Bill Aucoin (our manager) and Sean Delaney (a jack-of-all-trades who did everything from helping refine our stage moves and collaborating on songs to driving our van in the early days) had an amazing ability to make each person in the band feel he was the favorite. Which is terrific, because the bickering and the attention and the approval that four very needy babies needed would not allow anyone to be an actual favorite. Both Bill and Sean could make each band member feel that he was the best and most important, like he was the driving force or the most talented or the special one. If not for them, I don't think KISS would've survived. Bill in particular was excellent at playing parent to a bunch of guys who weren't much younger than him.

In earlier times, performing was my oxygen. It was my blood. Today, I love performing for different reasons. I still covet and cherish the attention and validation, but I don't depend on it anymore. I love it because I don't need it.

Somebody asked me recently, "Why do you still do it?"

"You know," I said, "being away from home is horrible. Going to sleep by myself in a hotel is horrible. But having that curtain go up and knowing that people have been waiting for the legend of KISS and what we embody to be with them for a night is so exhilarating—*that's* why I do it."

I do it because there's nothing to compare to being KISS, and I love it. I love what we are, I love what we create, and most of all I love the connection to the audience. When I started, I did it for myself. Now I do it for them. And it's made all the difference.

Early on, I didn't ever want to go home. Whereas now, I tolerate everything that goes along with being on tour—and being away from Erin and our kids—because being onstage is part of who I am, and my family has to understand it's a part of me. I don't have to do it, but I *want* to.

Maybe as the puzzle's gotten larger, the piece that KISS represents has gotten smaller. But it's still an essential piece of the puzzle. Nothing can measure up to being KISS onstage. Nothing can measure up to that outfit and being up there singing those songs or being there for the audience. At this point there really is a legend of KISS, and I'm grateful to be part of it.

I always say, "Show me a band that tells you they want to play clubs, and I'll show you a band that can't play an arena." They're both fun, but nobody's going to tell me they'd rather play multiple clubs or multiple auditoriums than play a stadium, an arena, or an outdoor festival ground. The energy is that much larger. I guess when people talk about electricity in the air, it has some real basis in physiology, because the energy that comes from an audience of 100,000 people can almost knock you off your feet. It's like a tidal wave. And to know that it's all there for you is incredibly empowering and exhilarating.

When the original four members of KISS reunited, there was, in my mind, a great sense of perhaps being able to fix things and come back smarter, with all of us appreciating who we are and where we'd been and picking up the flag and running. KISS without makeup was still making very, very good money, but nothing could compare to what we had done in our heyday.

When we put the makeup back on, I found that I was yearning for that level of success again. Not beforehand, oddly enough, but once I committed to doing it, I thought, *I'm going to savor this a lot differently than I did the first time.*

I was determined to appreciate it as an adult and take it in on all levels, which I hadn't done the first time around. That was palpable and emotional. Many nights, I choked up onstage.

Being able to revisit something with a deeper appreciation of it was a gift. Who gets the chance to do that? The first time, I hadn't lived enough or gone through enough to really see the success as part of a bigger picture. And then to see it again with a more mature eye was wondrous.

Now we've sustained it for decades again.

I still remember being backstage at the American Music Awards, with Tupac, when we were unannounced surprise guests, appearing with makeup for the first time in well over a decade. And I was back there thinking, *Is the audience going to laugh at us? Are they going to boo? Are they going to see it as a joke?*

Then we walked out, and every adult musician in the audience was reduced to being a kid again. The wonder on their faces was unbelievable. I mean, I can remember looking at some very famous faces that all of a sudden were transported. That was an incredible feeling—that we actually could go back, put on those outfits, put on the boots, put on the makeup, and be KISS. I didn't realize the magnitude, the importance to people, the impact we had had on people.

That first blush of returning and getting up early in the morning in Los Angeles to listen on the phone as Ticketmaster put tickets on sale and we sold out a show in a few minutes and rolled into a second show and a third show? That was a gift, and it was a gift to all of us.

When we sold out Tiger Stadium to kick off the tour, I was stunned. I hadn't realized how much we meant to people and how much they wanted us back. I guess no one really talked about it because maybe no one thought it was possible. And when it happened, it really was the second coming.

I only wish that everybody had realized that it could've been a new beginning. But that would've meant work.

I was prepared to appreciate it and savor it and feel blessed. And feeling that way obligates me to do something as well as I can—to be *worthy* of it.

Over time, unfortunately, not everyone saw it that way. Once we weren't firing on all cylinders, then we were KISS in name only. We weren't living up to our obligations to our fans and to ourselves. That was disappointing and demoralizing to a point where we really felt we needed to pull the plug.

But I love this band so much that it quickly became clear to me that I didn't want it to end. I just wanted the pain and the embarrassment to end.

It's been nice to reconnect with Ace in recent years, to sing on his album and have him on a KISS Kruise. It was terrific, but it doesn't mean any more than what it was. It wasn't a mating dance or anything. It was about enjoying the good part of our shared history, and maybe my being able to help him out. It was not going to lead anywhere except to our having a good time and my embracing somebody who has been very important in my life. Without Ace, there wouldn't have been a KISS. So isn't that worth celebrating and embracing?

Around the time of our induction into the Rock and Roll Hall of Fame, a reporter asked me, "For old time's sake, one more time, you wouldn't want to do that [perform together again]?"

I said, "How many times have you been married?"

"Twice," the reporter said.

"How about for old time's sake you go back and spend the night with your ex-wife?"

I think we came to an understanding at that moment.

To have Ace back in a larger capacity in my life is nice. The idea of having him on a KISS Kruise ten years ago would have been preposterous. There had been too many acrimonious feelings and unresolved issues—and just a lack of comfort. But life's too short. If Ace were a dick now, I wouldn't want him around. But if we can enjoy each other, we have too much shared magic not to.

Peter unfortunately is a different story. I don't think Peter has any life. He seems consumed by some kind of reality that his wife tells him. He's always been negative and always maintained an us-against-them mentality. I don't want that in my life. It's not about having differences, because I'm sure Ace and I have differences. It's Peter's overall sense of anger and resentment and feeling like a victim. He needs to acknowledge his participation and then change things. I think Peter's life is probably very one-dimensional, uninteresting, unstimulating—which is a result of seeing the world negatively and seeing everyone from the band members to the hotel service people as disrespectful.

That's not a world anyone should live in, and I don't want to be a part of it.

In the past few years, I began to realize that life is like dodge ball. In one form or another, we're just trying to make sure the ball doesn't hit us. And in the course of that, we watch people around us get knocked out. In our own way, we're all trying to duck the ball.

Sometimes the total picture of somebody is frozen in time when they die. They become talented and beautiful forever. Look at the difference between the living James Dean and Marlon Brando and the James Dean and Marlon Brando we think of now that they are gone. Kurt Cobain was clearly tortured from within, by mental illness and the manifestations of drug addiction. But who's to say that two albums later he wouldn't have been panned by every critic, and the people who loved him would have scratched their heads at the music he was making? Youth walks the high wire, and the lucky ones make it across. Some are predisposed to more risks, but I don't know that Kurt Cobain was anywhere near a point of being able to embrace himself, to love himself.

Fortunately, I'm more than content. I'm thrilled with life. My life has exceeded anything I ever could have hoped for. Only when we live and set goals and learn things along the way do we have any idea of what is possible. We have to experience life to know its potential.

What we exude, and what others see, is usually a product of what's inside us. I'm not the person I was five years ago. And certainly I'm not the person I was thirty years ago. I'm happier, more content, more likeable.

It's hard to be likeable when we're unhappy. Someone may take pity on us and, for their own reason, want to befriend us because it makes them feel better about themselves. I call that the Florence Nightingale syndrome. Some people like to find a person who's in worse shape than they are because it makes them feel better about themselves—it's comforting in an odd way, I guess.

Yet when someone is happy, people just want to be around that person—and perhaps want to know why they're happy.

15

VANITY ISN'T NARCISSISM

The better physical shape we're in, the better prepared we are to take on other aspects of our lives. When I'm in shape, I have better relationships. When I have better relationships, I eat better. These are all mini-mountains we can scale, and success at one motivates us to tackle the next.

Nobody wants to see a fat guy in tights. That fact first occurred to me shortly after I turned thirty. I still looked fit because of all the shows we played, which were physically and aerobically demanding. But cholesterol runs high in my family—I look at a steak and my cholesterol goes up. Growing up, the basic food groups were meat, cheese, whole milk, and eggs. Both my mom and dad had coronary bypasses, and my grandmother died of heart disease back when it was routinely a death sentence.

So I realized I would probably have to work at staying in shape going forward.

In the early 1980s, TV fitness gurus were all the rage. So, grasping at straws, I got a number for a guy who had a show called *Body by Jake*. It was the era of Arnold Schwarzenegger's ascent in Hollywood, and Jake was built like a brick shithouse.

I didn't want to look like that, but I called him to see about training. At some point during the conversation he said, "I'm going to make you hurt!" And I thought, *Why would I pay somebody to make me hurt?* Even then I knew that we don't measure how fit we are by how much we hurt—*I can't walk, so, boy, I must be doing great.*

He wasn't the guy for me.

Fortunately a friend of mine then referred me to another trainer named Michael Romanelli. He asked me what kind of shape I was in. I kind of scoffed and told him I was in better shape than 98 percent of the population. Once I truly started to get in shape, I realized that if I was in better shape than 98 percent of the population, the rest of the population was teetering on the edge of death. The good thing, though, was that Michael showed me there was really no secret to getting in shape. There was no need for a gym. No need for expensive equipment. Up to then, I had the common misperception that we need to rely on externals and intimidation by people who supposedly know more than we do and who get us to buy things or subscribe to things or sign up for things we really don't need. Bricklayers don't spend time in the gym. They lift bricks. Lifting your own weight is effective. Crunches don't take anything. So this can be broken down into something that's doable for everybody. With that in mind, I got in great shape.

That was thirty years ago. I'm in uncharted territory at this point: if you'd have told me back then that I'd still be running around in a spandex jumpsuit today, I would have asked what you were smoking. I won't tell you I'm the same person now that I was then. Nobody is immune to aging. Can I do as much onstage now as I once did? I would have to say no. But I do a lot. And I do far more than people in most other bands, even bands whose members are twenty-five years old, not sixty-five. To be in shape now validates my life and the quality of my life. To be onstage and feel relatively ageless is exhilarating. So these days, more than ever, I feel an intense desire to exercise. In fact, if I don't, it bothers me. Because when I do, I know that I've done my part.

Once you get started, the rewards of taking care of yourself continue to motivate you. When I first started working out, I didn't realize how out of shape I was until a few days into a workout when my body was really in shock. But that passes, and there's nothing more motivating than results.

After four weeks of working out, I looked in the mirror and got it. I understood what it was all about.

When you start working out, it's easy to wonder why you're doing it—there's the soreness and the inconvenience and the time it takes away from your day. But once you see results, whether that means losing pounds or inches or just feeling better, you want to do it more. I remember about a month in, I started to see and feel a difference. And I just wanted to keep going. It became something I put on my calendar and was nonnegotiable. It became time I wouldn't let be taken away for meetings or social events. It was my time. And it no longer seemed like a chore. It was more like an adventure.

In addition, endorphins are one of the strongest drugs in the world. When our endorphins are flowing, our minds are clearer. When our bodies feel fit and our minds are clear, we feel ready to take on the world. I've had times when I felt I could lift a building. Luckily I wasn't stupid enough to hurt my back and try, but there is a sense of being capable of anything.

Working out has become a priority in my life, knowing that anything I do to make myself better will ultimately help me in everything else I do. It became part of my commitment to bettering myself. One effective way to feel good about ourselves is to be in shape. It not only changes the chemistry of our bodies, it also changes how we view our bodies and ourselves more generally. It's all-encompassing. For me, it's also necessary. It requires a discipline to maintain who I am onstage, though quite honestly I'm vain enough to want to do it for myself, quite apart from how it helps me perform. A good friend of mine once wrote in a book that I was terribly vain. I thought, *How can I be terribly vain?* You're either vain or you're not—and I'm vain.

So I said to him, "I'm not terribly vain. I'm vain."

You're dead or you're not dead.

Being vain is different from being narcissistic. The whole basis of narcissism is the story of Narcissus wasting away or drowning by becoming obsessed with his own reflection. Well, that's a serious negative. But nobody should confuse narcissism and vanity. I'm proud to be vain. Who doesn't want to look their best?

Meanwhile, I don't want to waste away or drown.

As I learned how to stay in shape, I also realized there is more to it than just eating well and exercising. If all we gain is muscle mass, we gain nothing. If we are not working our minds and our hearts, we wind up being a car without an engine. It's great to start off a day reflecting on what we have done and what we want to accomplish or how we want to take on the world. And when we go to sleep, when we are lying in bed, we should be in a position to be grateful for the day gone by and to thank ourselves or whatever higher power we believe in for a valuable day of experience and another day spent getting closer to our goals.

I don't want to sound like Yoda, but our body and mind need to work in harmony. If we want to experience a life of the highest quality, making the most of all its possibilities, we need to take care of not only our bodies, but our minds, our souls. Ultimately, nothing will make us feel better about the world than helping it. Nothing will make us feel better about people than helping them. Generosity of spirit is necessary to live a positive life. I wake up every day and have a thought for what I want to get out of the day; at the end of the day I know I accomplished that goal or worked toward it. Without that, life is empty no matter what shape we're in.

Process leads to the completion of goals in life. It's all about process. We can't get from point A to point B without taking the first step. So the process—boring as it may seem—is actually exhilarating. I'm far from obsessed with working out. But it's necessary to elevate my quality of life. Committing to staying in shape also reinforces my ability to do something that I'm not always all that enthused about doing. But I know the process will lead to looking better, feeling better onstage, and standing taller.

Of course, we should never do anything until we're ready to do it 100 percent. There have been times when I didn't work out for a year. I wouldn't do that now, but I don't believe in doing things half-assed. If you're not going to commit yourself to something, then don't do it at all. When you're ready, jump in.

I'm not saying we have to devote all our energy to one thing. But we have to give 100 percent to whatever we're doing at any moment. Otherwise what's the point? If we read a book and we don't really focus on it, we have to read it again.

One of the motivating factors for this book came from the fact that I wish somewhere along the line somebody in my life had been more of a peer than a steroided-up muscle freak guiding me to good health. Honestly, even when I had trainers, it became apparent to me that how a trainer looks is a very clear reflection of how that trainer thinks *you* should look. That's key: if a trainer looks like he shits muscles, unless that's what you want to look like, you're with the wrong person.

My tendency is to get thick and bulky, so it's important for me to be careful not to lift heavy weights. And it was hard to explain that to a trainer. A few trainers would say, "Yeah, yeah, I understand." Then all of a sudden I'm looking in the mirror and seeing Lou Ferrigno.

At one point Bill Aucoin said to me, "You're not supposed to look like that," which is to say, my body had started to look like I was going to shave my chest and douse myself with baby oil.

So it's a matter of knowing from experience and then putting your foot down and saying, "This is what I'll do, and this is what I won't do." If you want a trainer, find one who looks like how you want to look—because that's how a trainer is going to try to make you look.

Body image is like anything else: it's personal. There's no right or wrong in terms of what you think looks good. I just happen to want my arms to touch my sides.

These days the heaviest weight I lift—ever—is ten pounds. As a rule, it's more like two or three pounds. And yet I've got the body I want—because of the repetitions. Unless you want to become Mr. America or star as Hercules, you want to work your muscles with repetitions, not heavy weights.

A lot of people make the same mistake I did—pushing themselves to see how heavy a dumbbell they can lift. Sometimes the dumbbell is the person trying to lift the dumbbell.

It's just that to most people—and to me in the beginning—the concept of high reps and low weights seems at odds with the idea of building muscle. But what we actually want to achieve is muscle fatigue. And muscle fatigue can come from either lifting a heavy weight a few times or lifting a light weight many times. I had to come to that realization.

Male bodybuilders tend to look like freaks in a suit because their lats are too big. They look like you put clothes on a gorilla. I remember my trainer, who had been a competitive bodybuilder, said the guy who wins a bodybuilding contest is the least healthy guy. The coming onto the scene of steroids and human growth hormones turned something that in theory was valid into something grotesque. Bodybuilding was initially a healthy approach to working out. Now, unfortunately, it's just a freak show. And it's not because of the workouts; it's because of how they're enhancing the workouts. When guys like that put on a suit, they look—I feel bad saying this—like they're trying to take a shit. Their necks look like they're about to explode.

I have always thought: *I don't want to look like that.*

Forget about competing in a Speedo. We have to wear clothes, and those body types don't look very good in clothes. I don't want to hurt anybody's feelings. This is just my take. But with few exceptions, when most people see us for the first time, we're clothed. So how our clothes fit and how they drape is a concern—even a priority. How do we look in clothes?

Getting out of them is a bonus. But we don't get a chance to get out of them with somebody unless first we're accepted when we're in them.

It's not what we accomplish lifting; it's how we lift and how we put the weight down. It's the control of the motion. That's how to get in shape. We get more out of the muscles when we use them from the beginning of a movement to the end. Lifting a weight is half of it. Bringing it down is the other half. And I'd rather do fifty curls with a five-pound weight than do five with a fifty-pound weight.

I've been doing the same workout for ten-plus years, and I have to say that when I found what I'm doing now, this cardio barre workout, I knew I'd found an all-encompassing workout. I don't even have to alter it when I'm preparing for a tour. I try to do it three or four times a week—not because I have to but because it feels great. It involves doing crunches, lifting light weights, doing extensions with my legs, twisting. Like anything else, when you find something you love—in my case an exercise regimen that I enjoy—it's more gratifying than debilitating.

There may be some hills and there may be some valleys, but once someone has the right plan, it goes back to what I say over and over: we'll be able to determine how important something is to us by how hard we're willing to work to achieve it. It's about determination.

Once we're ready to do it, it's pretty easy.

And fortunately it's never too late to get in shape. It's all relative. When somebody says that you look great for fifty, it doesn't mean you look great for thirty. And why should it? Looking great for fifty is enough in itself. Being in shape has made all the difference for me no matter how old I am.

Nobody can kid you and tell you that they're the same person they used to be. I'm not. But a seasoned fighter throws fewer punches while making each punch count. I make sure everything I do has impact—I've become a wiser fighter.

We all have to let go of any preconceived ideas we have about what getting older means, because that's usually based on a child's perception. It's not based on reality. It's based on what we supposed our parents were like at a given age. We somehow believed that our parents had all the answers. Then once we become parents, we realize that we're still kids trying to figure it all out.

At this point, being in shape validates my life and the quality of my life.

It's interesting to have young fans come to KISS shows and be blown away by how I look physically. And I've definitely seen wives elbow their husbands while mouthing, "He's older than you are!"

But there's no secret to it. And it's not an obsession. Or a chore. I can remember a time when I thought that people who worked out a lot had some kind of compulsion or almost a weakness that made them do it. But done the right way, it's neither of those things.

I didn't get to where I am overnight, but I'm here to tell you: once that engine is turned on and those pistons are chugging, there's no telling how long you can keep it on the road.

As you know, I've got three kids younger than age fifteen; I've met many of my friends through those kids. And that means that a lot of them are fifteen or twenty years younger than I am.

Most can't keep up with me.

We all play beat the clock and lose. Time always wins. But we can fight it in a way that's not embarrassing. We have to let go of preconceived notions about what it means to get older. And there's certainly no shame in trying to stay young.

I for one don't mind getting older, but I don't want to get old.

And so far it's working. KISS is still touring, hitting dozens of countries on five continents in recent years. The annual KISS Kruise has so far attracted fans from thirty-three countries. The KISS Army—and now Navy—is alive and well: what started out as a protest in front of a radio station in Terre Haute, Indiana, by kids upset that the disc jockeys wouldn't play the KISS songs they wanted to hear is now several generations deep. And all of this is possible because I can still perform at the physical level our shows demand.

Part of what keeps KISS immortal is that, for all intents and purposes, we look the same. We maintain the illusion.

I may not be ageless, but I am happy.

16

PRIDE IN WHAT WE DO IS PRIDE IN WHO WE ARE

'm not a risk-taker. I don't skydive. Why would I go up thousands of feet in the air and jump out when I'm already on the ground? That doesn't make sense to me. I've never thought I needed to risk my life to prove I'm alive.

But I do like ice cream—despite my family's cholesterol problem. In the 1980s—as I entered my thirties—I went to a doctor to have my levels checked for the first time in my life, and he said, "You can never eat ice cream again."

I said, "You're talking to the wrong guy."

Life doesn't work that way.

I don't want to eat a protein bar that tastes like Silly Putty and carpet shavings. Being healthy and eating fairly well doesn't have to mean compromising taste. Too many people see food as just fuel or an excuse to have an hour off from work. It's true that feeding ourselves is something we have to do several times a day, day in and day out. But it can be transformed into a positive aspect of our lives.

Food can be a sensory treat. It has aesthetic beauty. You can experience a meal. You can enjoy a meal. In America, though, we tend to shove food into our mouths like garbage. It's regarded as fuel as opposed to something worth savoring.

The thing is, it's something we have to do anyway—and elevating a daily necessity like that is edifying. By changing the experience, we change how we see ourselves.

I say: cook like you give a damn! It's another way to take pride in doing something right.

Anything worth doing is worth doing well. There's no point in attempting something without committing ourselves to it fully. Otherwise we sabotage the potential for it to succeed, and we also sabotage the potential for it to give us all that it can. We can only get out of something as much as we put into it. That means children. That means relationships. That means exercise. And that means food.

Everything.

Just a few days ago I made pasta for myself. It may seem like a weird statement and perhaps overblown for the situation, but I can't tell you how happy I was sitting down with that bowl of what's called cacio e pepe. It's spaghetti with ground black pepper, butter, and grated pecorino Romano. I sat in my kitchen by myself, just so happy.

It was a relatively simple meal, and yet there was satisfaction in having done it properly, and in knowing that I didn't take the path of least resistance. I could have just slapped together a sandwich. Instead, I'd provided an opportunity not only to feel good about myself but also to eat the rewards.

How cool is that?

Blandness and mediocrity are easy. It doesn't always take a lot of effort to elevate our sense of self. That bowl of cacio e pepe wasn't a tremendous effort, and yet it was an effort, and that effort made me enjoy the meal and feel better about myself in a fundamental way. If I had chosen not to make the dish, I would have sat there afterward and thought, "I should have and I could have." It would have been a waste: a waste of calories, sure, but perhaps most importantly a waste of an opportunity.

It's crazy, but that simple bowl of pasta was my life in a meal.

Doing that sort of thing gives us a sense of pride in ourselves. It's not necessarily something we have to share with others, although that's terrific too. It starts with us. The optimal way to enhance ourselves is not to look for approval or validation from the outside. It comes first from inside. It's nice to have it reinforced, but it's hollow unless we believe it ourselves.

It's no different with KISS—it's never been about someone else thinking we did a great show on any given night. It's never been about a great review for any given show. It's only about how I saw the show. The rest of it, and it may seem contradictory or hypocritical, is only of any value to me if it correlates with my own assessment. Otherwise, I discard it. If everybody around me says it was a great show and I didn't feel it, I'm left feeling hungry. I'm left feeling disappointed. It's much more fulfilling to base things on our own perceptions than on somebody else's. That's the same reason I ask my children to try to examine how they feel when they succeed at something, rather than simply seeking parental approval.

I once had a carpenter at my house working on a cabinet. I saw that he was doing really shoddy work, so I said to him, "Forget about what I think about it. How can *you* accept it? This is your work. This is your craft. Forget about me. What about you?"

When we do something, are we doing it for someone else or are we doing it for ourselves? If we get nothing back from someone else, what we get internally should make it worthwhile. The bonus is the external. The sense of self and knowing that we did a good job—knowing, for instance, that we're good parents, or that we're good people—should start with knowing we're living up to our own potential. Obviously the results will show in our children, in the path we choose, in the impact we have on the people around us, but we are defined by our successes as well as our attempts. Doing our best elevates our lives and the quality of our existence.

Even when we're by ourselves, do we want to eat slop, or do we want to create something that's a reflection of caring? If I make a great meal and no one else is there to share it with, the most important element of the satisfaction and validation has to come from me, not from those around me.

I came to cooking by necessity. When I started out, I didn't know the first thing about it. I just needed to make healthy food for my young son after his mother and I split up. I also wanted him to see that life goes on and that I would make sure everything was okay. Very quickly I found myself reaching a point where I no longer wanted to make food that fulfilled the basic need for nourishment but food that was pleasurable to eat and look at. And even though I didn't know how to do that, I had a pretty good idea how I might learn to.

In 1977, I went to London and visited a clothing store called Ebony. It was on South Molton Street, which was lined with cool shops. At the time, I was a horrible dresser. I wore clothes that looked as if I had borrowed them from Thomas Jefferson, and in terms of understanding how to dress, I was clueless. So I went into Ebony and picked up a sports jacket. I took it to one of the clerks and said, "I like this jacket. Can you pick a shirt that goes with it?" Then I asked him to pick out a pair of pants and a tie. I did the same thing another time, in another shop, and then I made myself a chart that had this shirt with that jacket and that tie. It seemed to make sense to me: I would write it down. I started to go shopping and look for things that were similar to, say, the shirt, and marked down on my chart that this new shirt could also go with that jacket and that tie. Then I started adding things. *Let's see, this sports coat is similar to the one I have, so I could wear it with these pants and this shirt.* After a while I was able to jettison the chart and to have confidence in my ability to choose. I created a style by starting with just two outfits and having a structure that allowed me to learn. I was methodical about it.

The same is true for how I learned to write songs. Initially I listened to songs I liked and tried to write one like it. *Oh, I like that song by the Who—I'm going to write one like it.* That went on even later, when, for instance, I wrote "Hard Luck Woman" after listening to Rod Stewart. I would hear something and absorb it and emulate it. "Hotter than Hell" was my "All Right Now," by Free. The templates for my songwriting were the people I admired, the people who inspired me. Over time, if you're good, you can transform those inspirations into something new. It's a question of taking different ingredients and turning them into something that's familiar, but not a copy of any of them. If, as a singer, I could transform a love of Sam Cooke, Steve Marriott, and Robert Plant into a style of my own, why couldn't I do the same with food?

And I did. Step by step. A process. I learned some basic building blocks and perfected a few dishes that allowed me to broaden my repertoire over time. But it all started with one dish and one step.

One of the first things I started to get good at was making meatballs. Anybody can make a meatball—it's just a lump of meat, after all. All you have to do is take some ground meat and roll it into a ball. But then I began to wonder: *How can I improve it? How do I elevate it?* Then I remembered my mom's meatloaf. Most people grow up despising meatloaf. That's because it's often just a five-pound hamburger. But my mom was smart enough to use a mix of different meats and different proportions of fat to meat to create a different flavor profile. When I first said to my kids I was going to make meatloaf, without even knowing what it would taste like, just from watching television, they thought I might as well be feeding them cockroaches. But as soon as they took a bite, it became one of their favorite things to eat.

So what's a meatball? A ball of meat. That's where it starts. But then you go from there. I wanted to learn how to improve it, create different textures and flavor profiles. Luckily my friend and chef extraordinaire Rocco DiSpirito gave me *his* mama's recipe, which was a road map to perfection. Committing to doing something challenging is incredibly satisfying. If we treat what we do as a craft or an art form, it enhances the people around us.

Even though I originally started cooking for a very simple, uncomplicated reason—to feed my son Evan—it led to my seeing that cooking can be a means of exploration, and that exploration can be gratifying. The joy I get from Emily loving my pasta with peppers and onions or Colin and Sarah's love of my frittata elicits an almost childish pride in me. Oftentimes we can initially do something for one reason, and the reward we get is not the intended one. Or it's more than the intended one. It fulfills the original need but then opens other doors that we couldn't have gotten to otherwise.

For example, had I not done *The Phantom of the Opera*, I wouldn't have written a book. Because not only did *Phantom* fulfill a decade-old yearning to do theater in general and

The Phantom of the Opera in particular, but also when I did it, I suddenly realized why it was that important to me, which I had been clueless about. It was so obvious, once I started doing it, what the connection was. *Phantom* led to my working with children with facial differences and their parents. None of that would have been possible otherwise. I never would have revealed my microtia to anybody. I had to do *Phantom* first, and then those doors—which I never would have found otherwise—opened.

When we commit to doing something, there's no way for us to know where it'll take us. Then we have to be receptive to possibilities and the doors that open. Most of the time, they're going to be doors that we couldn't even see beforehand.

Food is not unlike art or music. We don't have to do it well to appreciate it. Because someone goes to a museum and looks at art doesn't mean that person can paint, but it shouldn't stop them from trying. The same is true with music. I remember listening to songs ten, twenty, a hundred times, trying to understand what was connecting me to the song. I listened over and over to figure out what was layered in there—which is the same way I try to figure out how something is cooked: I try to discern the layers.

Painting started out as a way for me to purge, to let out a lot of pain and turmoil. But it turned into something incredibly joyous. Quite honestly, it's surprising to me how much I love some of my pieces. That's something I never, ever could have imagined. I never could have imagined that my art would affect other people either. And most of all, I never could have imagined looking at some of my art and thinking that if I saw it in a gallery, I would love it.

Every time I take on a challenge or I become interested in going down a new avenue, I learn something about myself. It's another piece of a puzzle that I didn't realize was so big or complex. But that complexity is rewarding.

Over the past twenty-plus years, I've steadily become more appreciative of culinary skills and the artistry of being able to cook, which shouldn't be confused with actually being able to do it. But in our own way we can use whatever skills or imagination we have to try.

There's nothing wrong with being proud that you boiled water for the first time. Everything starts at step one. We can't get to step twenty if we don't start somewhere. Success starts with trying. God knows I've made enough food that I took a bite of and threw away, but it hasn't stopped me. It showed me that I did something wrong. I try to be my own harshest critic and to learn from my culinary mistakes as much as I learn from all my mistakes.

Erin's love of baking and my love of cooking have sparked a can-do kitchen adventure for all three of our young ones, which has them inventing their own culinary creations. Being creative in our house is so much the norm, and the idea of can-do as opposed to can't-do is so much a part of our day that it has been both amusing and fulfilling to have Colin and

Sarah, who are both amazingly athletic and terrific students at school, also take such a liking to food and to cooking.

One day I was in the kitchen just as Colin was pulling from the oven some sugar cookies he had baked from scratch. He announced very matter-of-factly that he and Sarah were going to make a Granny Smith apple pie. I smiled, but also sensed possible disaster. Even so, their curiosity and obvious commitment to doing it were so palpable that both Erin and I said, "That's great!"

They told us they were going to make the pie crust from scratch, which in itself would be challenging. And then they started cutting up apples. Erin and I left them alone for hours. And lo and behold, when we came back downstairs, there was a beautiful apple pie. It even had latticework on the top. We were stunned.

That pie took me back to my making pants for Gene and myself when we played the Hotel Diplomat in 1973. My parents told me that they appreciated my tenacity, but they thought making those pants was pretty much impractical and out of reach. Mind you, I managed to make two great pairs of pants, even though every step of the way—from cutting the fabric to putting in the zippers—I was told it would be impossible. My parents appreciated my effort, but they didn't think it would come to anything.

The difference with my children is that Erin and I cheer them on. And now, here was this beautiful apple pie in front of us. When Colin and Sarah asked us to sit down to have a piece, Erin and I looked at each other like, *Now the fun stops.* Then I took a bite of it. It was mind-blowing. And I told them that. I said, "I would be proud if I'd made this—it's amazingly good!" Which was followed quickly by Erin saying, "And you kids are making the pies for Thanksgiving!"

Their sheer can-do spirit, coupled with a naivety about what is possible, brought the results that maybe in some ways mirrored my success with the band and Erin's success as an attorney.

Perhaps when we don't know how difficult something is going to be, it isn't that difficult after all. We can use whatever skills or imagination we have—and then just try.

I'm certainly not a chef. But I like cooking the way a chef might like playing guitar. It doesn't make the chef a rock star, and liking to cook doesn't make me a chef. But I take joy in being able to feed my family and myself and make nice food. Cooking turns a house into a home, because eating food we make ourselves fills the shell of a house with the life of a home.

With cooking, I kept adding fundamental skills—like deglazing a pan, which is a fancy term for pouring some liquid, usually some form of alcohol, into a frying pan and making sure you scrape up all the flavorful bits of food clinging to the bottom so that flavor infuses whatever it is you're cooking rather than just making the pan tough to scrub out later. I needed someone to open a door for me. If we can find some-body to help us, it's foolish not to take the help. The only dumb question is the one we don't ask. There's so much experience around us that to close our ears and make believe we know everything only hurts us. In my case, I started messaging chefs through Twitter and asking them questions. That's how I learned to deglaze my pan with some Marsala wine and chicken stock to get the concentrated flavors in the bottom of the pan.

I once tried to make a pasta dish with chicken and peas, and it seemed easy enough, but when I tasted the results, it was unremarkable. In that instance I messaged Rocco DiSpirito. What was the problem with the dish? Turns out it starts at the beginning. You have to build what they call a *sofrito*. You have to build your flavors at the beginning with your herbs, with your stock. You have to deglaze your pan. Without the fundamentals, you can't make a great dish.

God is in the details. God is also in the nuances. It's those subtleties we miss that make something great. At a restaurant recently I had to remark that something I was eating was just heavy-handed. And yet those same ingredients in the right hands would have been in proportions that worked. Maybe food is no different from anything else in life. It's all about proportions. It's all about what takes the lead and what supports it. And though I'm far from being a chef, it's the little things I can learn that become the building blocks to something else, whether it's building a wardrobe from one jacket, one shirt, and one pair of pants or building up a recipe collection by starting with one dish.

Suddenly, with help, I had a good dish. And then I realized I could do something similar with shrimp—and just like with my jacket-shirt-tie chart, I was off to the races. I've got a long way to go, but as naive and elementary as it sounds, that is so exciting to me. I made this pasta with chicken and chicken stock and Marsala wine, I did it right, and it was the key that opened a door that had been closed.

That sort of thing—a basic accomplishment like making an awesome pasta dish—is exciting. I would have been chasing my tail, but a little bit of knowledge and guidance started me on another journey. Armed with that knowledge and guidance, I've been able to put a personal stamp on the food in my home. I'm not making Michelin-star dishes, but I'm making good, tasty food.

And I'm not skipping dessert, Doc. I mean, is there a good substitute for ice cream? Fuck no. So eat the ice cream. And enjoy it.

For myself, I'll have my ice cream and then figure out something else to sacrifice. But if I'm going to have dessert, I want the real thing. Some things can't be replaced, and there's no reasonable facsimile of ice cream.

Also, certain savory dishes just need fat. You simply can't make certain foods with lean meat. You have to have the fat. A good hamburger has to have 20 to 30 percent fat. The discipline we have in what we *don't* eat allows us the freedom to eat what we *do* eat. There really is a way to do it without feeling that we have to eat sawdust to be healthy.

Some things just can't be replaced. Eat the ice cream. That's what life is about.

17

IF WE KEEP MOVING FORWARD, WE NEVER FINISH THE JOURNEY

At this point, I've reached the mountaintop in the field of music. But I want to replicate the high. There's a hunger to find another means of replicating that feeling of accomplishment and validation. I don't think that goes away.

That feeling of getting to know another side of yourself and getting to see what you're capable of is built on your prior accomplishments. Any of the guys who originally went into space as astronauts had to start out as student pilots, after all.

Our successes open doors to other possibilities, and we want to get the same psychological rush of fulfillment, if not the same adrenaline rush, of seeing what we're capable of.

I'm always looking to see what more I'm capable of. Not because of any feelings of inferiority, but because it enhances what's already there. At this point in my life, it helps to broaden the picture, add to the mosaic. It helps to create a bigger sense of who I am. And it's uplifting, if only because I surprise myself by what I can do.

We all can surprise ourselves by what we can do.

When you achieve success, some people will try to intimidate you, but for God's sake, don't intimidate yourself.

That's a mistake many people make: they intimidate themselves and don't let themselves experiment.

The joy of creating something tangible from the intangible is one of the most gratifying experiences I have in life. Any outlet that I've found for expressing myself has helped me to define myself. So from the very beginning, as soon as I picked up a guitar, I wanted to write songs. I wanted to express myself. If for no one else but myself, I wanted to hear my own thoughts. In writing books, I wanted to express my own thoughts. In painting, I wanted to see my own thoughts. All vehicles for interpretation.

It wasn't always that way for me—I rejected art as a path back in high school.

From an early age, I sketched and drew at home, and quite honestly I couldn't understand why nobody else could draw as well. I would look at something, and while I looked at it to draw it, my eye would connect to my hand. It was second nature. By the time I got to school, I was very comfortable with my artistic ability. When I was in grade school, we used to do an assignment they called a product map, which was a map of a state showing the state's industries. It would be done on a large piece of oaktag—that's what we called it—like poster board. The boards would be about three feet by three and a half feet, and every kid dreaded having to do them. But it took me only five minutes—I could just look at a map of a state and draw an enlarged version freehand.

Despite my comfort with my artistic ability, over time I found myself not ultimately committed to it. I just wasn't motivated enough, and I guess that goes back to not being excited enough. I wasn't eager enough to put in the time. Hence, when I got to the High School of Music and Art—which I commuted from Queens into Manhattan to attend—I encountered people who were not only as good as me but far better. That only made me that much more committed to music, which is something I never stopped working at.

I've never been good at taking direction. I've never been good at dealing with authority figures. I've never been good at working to someone else's schedule. However, nobody works harder, is more motivated, or can deliver more dependably than I can. But outside of what I *choose* to do, I'm not very good at bending to other people's rules.

I don't think it's a coincidence that most of the great modern painters, before they went into abstract phases, learned the techniques of painting realistically. For those artists, it was a calling. It was something they felt compelled to do. And the way for many of them, I guess, was they started in art school and under tutelage. I totally understand that, and it is probably what makes their work so timeless, deep, and great. That being said, I'm not of that school. While I find all those great artists inspiring, I don't have the time, patience, or wherewithal to backtrack. I was not an aspiring artist.

I've come back to art as a diversion, as a place where I can express myself without being judged or thinking about anyone's expectations. So I'm coming to it now from a different place. Painting, untrained as I am, fulfills a need in me, and the creative outlet is satisfying as it is. I've never been somebody who does things by the book, and I'm also aware that I will never be a Picasso, which is just fine.

This doesn't mean that my art can't affect somebody as much as a great artist's work can. It's definitely gratifying when someone connects to one of my paintings. But I don't have the foundation or schooling that contemporary artists do now. When I started painting again, I had no guidance, and I liked that a lot. It may seem like I'm contradicting myself, but I've enjoyed the purity of figuring it out on my own. It's important for each of us to know what we are and who we are, and not try to be something we're not—it's something that applies to all areas of life. I'm never going to be a master artist. It would be pointless to try. I can't do that. And yet, doing it the way I do, putting in real effort and passion even while I'm aware of my limitations, works.

It's crazy to look for perfection or not settle for less than perfection—because we'll always be unhappy. The truth is, we're not settling for less; we're dealing with reality. I realized in the past twenty years or so that nothing in life is perfect. If we accept the imperfection in life, we see things more realistically. Happiness comes from accepting imperfection and determining how to deal with it.

It's not negative to say that the world is imperfect, that relationships are imperfect, that life is imperfect. If we embrace this, we remove the desire for an ideal that will always leave us dissatisfied. We're not lowering the bar. We're accepting reality. That's a good thing.

The world is beautiful despite imperfection—or even because of it.

Of course, life intervenes in other ways too. We're all faced with deadlines to one degree or another, as well as obligations or responsibilities that are part of everyday life. For me, the idea of creating on a schedule or on demand—which was how it worked at the art school—seemed contrary to creativity. In part, that was due to my counterproductive pursuit of perfection. But certainly as an adolescent and a teen I didn't want something that I did out of spontaneity and a sense of freedom to suddenly be harnessed.

Over time, with music I found that spontaneity could work. But we can't become prisoners to inspiration; we have to use it as a tool. If we just wait around to be inspired, we'll probably do a lot less—and we'd be a whole lot less creative.

Early in KISS's career, our business manager told me we needed to go in and do another album—that I had to write songs, and quickly.

I said, "Well, I'm not really feeling inspired right now."

And he said, "I'll show you your bills, and you'll get inspired."

The trick is to manage both inspiration and creativity without compromising either—I certainly want to be proud of whatever I do, but I also want to keep the creative juices constantly flowing.

The reason I don't have a lot of unrecorded songs around is because at some point in the creative process I didn't believe they were good enough. Once I start to explore an idea, be it a riff or a chord pattern, if it's worth pursuing, I'll go on to a melody. But if it's not, I'll chuck it. In the course of writing the melody and lyrics, I'll listen and think *This isn't good enough*, and get rid of it. It seems pointless to complete something I know isn't up to my standards when I could be spending that time doing something of value. I've become much better at it. In the early days, I would go further before abandoning ideas. They say "Old too soon, smart too late." As we age, it becomes clearer that the time we spend on something is time we can never get back.

Time becomes more precious as it marches on. This goes back to the conveyor belt of life. We never get back the time it takes to complete something that we know isn't great—just as we never get back the time wasted on a dead-end relationship.

What's the point of pursuing something if it's only an exercise in mediocrity? It's a waste of time.

In the old days, I had hours of tape of almost stream-of-consciousness applied to music, just letting my hands go and seeing what came out. But I would record over the tapes. Even now, when there's basically unlimited capacity to record,

I work the same way. Because more important than storage capacity is time.

Time truly is the one thing we can't buy.

Everything I do creatively sparks my need and necessitates my taking the next step. So whether it's songwriting or art or anything else, every piece I do spurs me to the next. And nothing that I'm doing today could I have done a year ago or five years ago or ten years ago. The excitement is the inspiration I get from something I did yesterday, which pushes me to what I can do today—often something that I couldn't have conceived of or possibly created yesterday. It's a constant process of evolution that builds on itself.

There was a time when I felt let down at the end of a tour or at the end of an album because I'd worked so hard to open up those creative channels and then they were going to close and I would in some ways have to start from square one again. Once something is moving, once it's rolling along, momentum will keep it going, and having to stop it for any reason means having to start it again from being still. What I've found is that at this stage in my life, keeping those creative channels open almost accelerates the progress. When I ski, I have to be careful about gaining momentum and picking up speed, but nobody ever got a concussion from painting or writing a song.

Once we open a faucet and let any undrinkable, rusty water run out, we have the opportunity to keep it flowing. And the more it flows, the less chance we have of going back to that stagnant situation. It's all intertwined, and the same laws apply to everything. Creativity, sense of self—it's all tied together, and it all builds on itself. Keeping my creative juices flowing, just like keeping my emotions flowing, affects my outlook and how I deal with people every day.

When the taps are open, we can see things differently. We can let go of old notions, old opinions, old ideas. As our vision becomes clearer, the screen becomes bigger. What becomes important in relationships and what no longer matters changes, because when we are fulfilled in different ways, we place less importance on some of the things that had importance to us previously. Misplaced importance in relationships or misplaced priorities can recede and become irrelevant as we find outlets that enrich us and define us.

As for the practical elements, to be our most creative, we need to be able to turn wherever we are into a solitary space. The substance of more creativity is always there because it's within us. It's within me. And the only variable from person to person is how much what goes on around us sabotages our ability to get to it. Some people need a cabin in the woods with birds singing and a babbling brook, but I don't believe it has to do with location; it has to do with mindset. If we can immerse ourselves in what we're doing and lose ourselves, then it's just a matter of whether or not our environment allows us to do that. We don't become inspired because we're away from home, nor do I think we become inspired just *because* we're home. Ultimately, any location can result in obstructions or roadblocks. We have to get rid of those as much as possible so we can lose ourselves and allow inspiration to come from inside.

I try to put the same sort of effort and inspiration into everything. I'm not aspiring to become a professional chef, and I'm not aspiring to make painting my primary job; yet I still find value in putting energy into those things. It's essential because what I've found and what has been reaffirmed over the years is that every time I find another means of self-expression, I'm that much happier—I find life that much more exhilarating.

The reason I've gone back to painting, after initially rejecting drawing and other forms of visual art, is that painting is more multileveled: I'm dealing with textures and colors and different types of application. So it turns out to be a more fulfilling and all-encompassing sense of expression. Sketching became very one-dimensional, whereas painting—at least for me—feels like a much deeper means of expression because of the complexity.

I paint with vibrant colors and I paint without any real foundation of color relationships. Does a field of wildflowers know anything about color relationships? No, but it all somehow works and affirms the beauty of harmony through diversity. I paint with spirit. Color affirms life. And the more I paint—the more that point of view manifests itself in my paintings—the more I see it as true. The more I paint and visualize how I see life, the more it becomes true.

And as far as being able to conceive of things differently today than I did yesterday, I see the colorful aspect of my painting affecting other aspects of my life. I recently made amazing campanelle pasta with sausage and broccoli rabe and toasted panko crumbs. It was off the charts. For some reason, up to that point I had overlooked one of the basic rules of cooking vegetables: keep vegetables like broccoli vibrant in color. This time, after I blanched the broccoli rabe, I put it in ice water, and it retained its bright green color. Now my food looks like my paintings. And if and when I write songs again, I will bring to my music everything that I've done since last I wrote.

I have absolutely no doubt that the music will have color.

The beauty of creative outlets is that they allow us to make a tangible manifestation of our outlook, and when we do creative work, we validate that outlook. When we make beautiful music or beautiful art, the world is more beautiful. Though, of course, we have to start somewhere, and it's not always from a beautiful place. When I first started painting, for instance, some of my early creations were almost like exorcisms—I needed to get that out to move on. The process of doing it was a cathartic way to move forward. I would want to hang myself if twenty years later I was painting the same images. But it was a way to purge, a way to acknowledge and face how I was feeling, a way to make a reality out of an emotion and look at it. It wasn't how I wanted to feel, but sometimes we have to acknowledge and validate where we are to move on. Those early paintings raised a lot of hard feelings in me, and yet today, I see them as beautiful—because they're a mile marker of where I was compared to where I am. Not unlike going to my old street in Washington Heights and seeing my old apartment. There's where I was—look at me now. The downside, the hurt, is gone; I can see how far I've come.

I can see similar examples when I look back at songs from the past. Generally speaking, I was uncomfortable with the KISS album *Carnival of Souls*. My issue with it was that I had never wanted to write songs reflecting dissatisfaction and unhappiness, or looking at the world negatively. Putting on a hat of misery felt fake and disingenuous—because of my belief in fighting through things, because of my fundamental optimism. In the midst of this artificial doom and gloom and the personal turmoil of my looming divorce, I did, however, have a creative epiphany I could apply. I realized that the only person I could swear I would always be there for was my flesh and blood: Evan. So there's one song on that album—"I Will Be There"—that affirmed my commitment to my child and also pretty much acknowledged that although other things were going to change, that one thing wouldn't. Now I can look at that mile marker and see that I kept that promise to my child—even through my personal trials and tribulations.

My current musical side project, Soul Station, is another type of creative outlet—one of those why-versus-why-not scenarios. The original idea was to be able to hear some of my favorite music and to have a band unlike any I'd ever had before, with every possible ethnicity and every possible background, with horn players and singers and two keyboard players, and this great diversity all held together by a passion for the music—vintage soul and R&B. It's been so invigorating, so joyous, and we love it so much. To establish this commonality in celebration together is another amazing affirmation of what we're all capable of doing. These people have individually played with everybody. Getting to know these people, who under other circumstances I would never have met, and laughing and eating and practicing together—it's a miracle.

Of course, everyone has these sorts of opportunities in one way or another, and we either shut them down or take advantage of them. Not that everybody has to have a Soul Station, but everybody has desires, and either we live with later saying "I wish I had . . ." or we do it. It's another example of how much richer our lives can be when we embrace and go for something.

Soul Station offers the chance to hear songs that I love, that are so much a part of my foundation and musical fabric, played live and spirited and with such joy and commitment. It would be great enough just to listen to the music, but to be a part of it is incredible. To be a participant and to be a part of this creation is exhilarating. And not only are people blown away by it and the authenticity of it, but I'm blown away by the joy of being a part of it. Like in many other things I've done in my life, I didn't understand the scope of what I could get back from attempting something new or from seeing it through.

It not only gives me a validation of the beauties in life but also has given me a new village. It has given me band members I never knew, and their friendship and their support, and they look at me the same way.

In life, we look for externals instead of trying to find ways to get to the internal. At the end of the day, the sense of belonging and knowing who we are and where we are, and that we're loved and valued, is the core of a much more fulfilling life. We can experience that in so many different ways. This incredible band of musicians from diverse backgrounds, who joined me in this quest to pay homage to a music that's so important to all of us, has become one way. And on top of that, we get to experience one another, socialize, have dinners together. I cook for them. We're all embracing each other. We're all getting something from one another that makes each one of us more fulfilled and more complete.

If I hadn't taken the steps leading up to the eventual creation of Soul Station, I would have never gained this experience. Everything starts with a first step, and where that first step takes us is what makes it so exciting. Originally I was doing a fundraiser for my kids' school, and I had put together a great band doing classic rock covers. The following year, I thought I would love to do those songs—since my roots are as much in Philly soul and Motown as in British rock. I made some phone calls and put together a band. It was so much fun that over the course of a year or so, it developed into Soul Station—a bona fide touring band.

So the first step was allowing myself to do something that people around me were skeptical about. When I told the sound people who worked with KISS that I was going to do a Motown-Philly R&B band, they said, "Who's going to sing?"

And when I said, "I'm going to sing," they looked at me like I was out of my mind.

Well, after the first show, they said, "Dude, we were wrong."

Rod Stewart said the same thing to me: "Who's singing?"

"Me," I said.

And he said, "You can handle those songs?"

As I played Rod a live recording, his jaw dropped and he broke into a wide grin and said, "Wow!"

Why not?

Giving ourselves the license to do something is the start. Like everything else that I've accumulated and done in my life, I can't imagine *not* having Soul Station any more than I can imagine not painting, any more than I can imagine not cooking. You just go down the list. All these things have become essential to who I am.

That's what everyone needs to find for themselves. We don't know what all it could be unless we give ourselves the license to explore. If you're considering exploring something new, do it! You have much more to gain than you do to lose.

If we don't do it, we live with regret. I'd rather live with failure. Because even failure can lead somewhere else. Doing nothing leads nowhere.

One thing people seem to hear a lot at KISS shows of late is, "Gee, I've never seen Paul smile so much. I've never seen him have so much fun onstage."

It's true. I bring that same joy to KISS.

I'm dead serious about what I do in the band, and I give it 100 percent of what I have, which may not be the same as 100 percent forty years ago, but the joy of being up there, the joy of playing with those guys, the joy of every other aspect of my life means I get to bring all that onstage with KISS. It makes it better. It makes it deeper and gives people a much more well-rounded sense of the band. It's less one-dimensional. There's a human being who's exhilarated and basking in that moment.

Everything I do is a celebration of life. Everything I do is a validation of my potential. Painting is a celebration of life because it's a validation of a creative outlet, of taking the intangible and making something tangible. Doing theater was a celebration of life because it affirmed the potential that we all have to explore different sides of ourselves. KISS is the same thing. I don't really distinguish.

How we live is a celebration of life—or should be. All that I'm involved in, and all the passion and energy I put into these things, affirms life in general.

I'm in awe of life.

When KISS started, it wasn't a celebration of life as much as a celebration of the right to be yourself and to follow your dreams. It wasn't about rebellion for rebellion's sake, but about fighting the status quo, fighting the system. But we could only do that for so long. Once we succeeded on a big scale, then it became a celebration of life. We became the living proof that you can believe in yourself, work against the system, and win. That's what KISS celebrates at this point. And if we can do it, you can do it.

Earlier in life, many of us might be more robotic, more like automatons. But eventually we become more human. Maybe one of the reasons I feel younger than I am is because I feel like I was born later than I was actually born. My childhood was lived at an older age. Yeah, I don't feel sixty-seven. Perhaps because so many of the things that I find most rewarding started late.

It's almost not fair to say that I feel young, because when I was young I didn't have these positive sensations. I live more now. Back then, I was young in age, but my spirit was old or broken.

As corny as it sounds, my life is filled with wonder. That's the reality of it. The excitement is never-ending. I never know where it will go next. And living this way is a conscious decision—and that's the important takeaway from this book.

I always like when people are surprised by something I do and say to me, "What's next?" I have no idea. But those new challenges are the things that define each of us. Maybe today we aren't aware of where we're going to go or what we're going to do. But that's how we get to know who we are—by the unanticipated challenges we take on, by the things we embrace, and by how we deal with them.

How do we define ourselves? The more things we do, the more goes into that definition. I'm very, very grateful and feel incredibly fulfilled by creative outlets I had never even considered, which makes me think I have no idea what's next.

Can I see the end? Sure. As I've said, life is like a conveyor belt, and I can remember having everyone in front of me. Now I can see that most people are behind me. That's coming to grips with our own mortality and the fact that when we're younger, life seems infinite. We can't conceive of it ending.

When it starts to seem finite, people sometimes find God. It's inconceivable for many people to think of the world continuing without them, so they have to believe—rightly or wrongly—that they're going somewhere else after they die. I certainly can't say whether or not that's true, but it's very much human nature for people to believe that the world revolves around them.

I believe in God, but not because I have any notion of going anywhere after I'm done here. The concept of God— whatever that is to each person—simply makes the world more beautiful. I don't know what God is, I don't know where we are, but believing in God gives me some sense of grounding and wonder.

One of the things that's been staggering to me is that fans who are in the final stages of their lives often want to connect with me. It's humbling, though grasping the magnitude of it is also difficult. About eighteen months ago I got a call from a woman whose friend was married to a gentleman who was in his last days of life. He was a huge KISS fan. He'd been a chef at a restaurant out here. I went to their house to sit with him. It was tough to face the reality that this amazing life and this man's plans, which, I'm sure, were as long-range and as far-reaching as mine, were in their final stages. I sat with him and told him that no one could tell him what he needed to do, that I was there with him and that I believed we'd meet again.

Whenever I've met people who are dying, I always feel the need to tell them that it's up to them to decide what happens next and that, for whatever it's worth, I support them in that. The idea that someone would get joy or hope or strength from me is such a gift. I certainly never got that. It's hard to articulate how stirring it is to be able to give someone that just by being.

A few years ago someone called me and told me that a young man in a hospital wanted to speak to me. I called him and told him that he was in my prayers and I supported him. This isn't anyone else's fight but yours, I told him, and you have to decide where you are in this battle. If you feel it's time to let go, no one knows but you, and nobody can tell you but you. If it means anything to you, I support your decision.

I called back a few days later, and his mother said he had just waited to hear from me and then he passed away.

There's no endgame. There's no point of arrival. There's no finish line.

I always picture death as going through swinging doors on a stretcher. You go in, and you never come out. That's when, as far as I know, it ends. I'm going to live every moment up until then. That's the only finish line that doesn't lead to another. Other than making wise decisions about health or safety, that's the one I have no say in. But up until then, I do have a say in what goes on. And I'm going to make sure that I'm smiling right up until the end.

OUTRO

Some KISS fans may be doctors and some may need doctors, but they're all united in their common love of KISS. The lengths to which members of the KISS Army and KISS Navy go to show their allegiance are legendary. And when they tattoo my Starchild face on their bodies, it's humbling. It points to my responsibility—my commitment must be worthy of theirs.

That might sound cheesy, but it's what got me this far: a belief in myself, a standard I owe to the people who put me where I am as well as to myself, and a joy in doing what I do.

KISS has always been the underdog, and the band champions those like us. We hope to inspire people through our accomplishments; we have always been relentless in pursuing our goals, and the audience can sense the genuine nature of our passion. It's at the core of everything I do, over the course of more than 2,500 concerts. I've thrown myself into every show. There is no substitute for a performer's commitment, no way to fake it.

And the same is true in life.

We have to do things properly—never lowering the bar. I suppose we can find ways to fool other people, but ultimately this undermines our own view of ourselves. If we don't do a job as well as we can, it's hard to look in the mirror. I owe myself better. You owe yourself better. We all owe ourselves better. And there is a reward in doing things properly: we build up a sense of self and take home a great feeling when we've given our best.

As I've said, nothing of any value comes without work, and we find out how important something is to us by how hard we are willing to work to achieve it. But I had to figure out *how* to work toward goals—and I've found that everything is accomplished incrementally. A clean room starts with one thing being picked up. And that's the most effective way to deal with life: look at what needs to be done, and then start with doing one thing.

What's great about starting to work on something and doing one thing at a time—whether it's getting in shape or launching a business—is that the task becomes much less overwhelming. If I had known how long it was going to take me to become a good guitar player, I never would have picked up the instrument in the first place. Or when I look at a tour itinerary and see one hundred shows: I break out in a sweat. *How am I ever going to do this?* Well, I do it one show at a time—one single show, one hundred times. The same was true for me with therapy: I went to therapy to get some answers. That was forty years ago. If I had realized that I was going to have to figure out the answers myself and that there was no quick fix, I probably would have just gotten high instead.

Or take surgery. I don't fear it, because I can't start working toward my goal of recovery until I get past the surgery. I see injuries as minor setbacks to living my life to the fullest. As long as we keep going forward, at some point we will turn around and see where we started. The first day sucked. The first week sucked. But here I am with two weeks behind me! Whether it's surgery or anything else, I look forward to having it happen because then it's one day behind me. I'm one day closer to the goal. We can't do anything that we're not willing to start.

KISS is a tribe at this point, and unlike most bands that are very age and demographic specific, we don't have a stigma. If a fan's younger brother or sister shows up, if the fan's father or mother shows up, if the fan's grandmother or grandfather shows up, it's all good. It's about being a member of the biggest cult in the world, of a secret society that is life changing, life affirming, and something you ultimately want to share. We are multigenerational and proud of it. KISS has long been heralded as "the people's band" because of the community we have created and the spirit of celebration that infuses all that we do.

We don't preach, we inspire.

Which is a long way of saying I've been successful by being an everyman. I think people look to me for inspiration because they see their attributes and their flaws in me, just as they see them in themselves. Meaning, if I can do it, perhaps everyone can—with a little guidance and support. That also explains why this book is a total package. Because what I've found is that it's not about what we can accomplish; it's more about how we can accomplish it.

In my case, I don't attribute my success to a certain way of working out or eating any more than I attribute it to positive thinking. Those things are part of it, of course, but what it's really about is a point of view—a way of facing the day, a way of taking control of my life.

I try to apply the same determination and passion even in areas some might dismiss as trivial. Some people might not think it helps us professionally to cook up a nice meal at home, for instance. But it does: everything is connected, and when we affect one thing, we affect everything—we raise the level of everything we do.

The KISS rider—the list of things promoters are contractually obligated to have for us backstage—has changed a lot over the years. Early on we used to order champagne by the case. Then we switched to Dr. Pepper. Our rider these days is surprisingly dull. The only drug anyone wants backstage is Advil. But part of the reward of success should be hard-earned knowledge, lessons learned, realizations and epiphanies across many aspects of life, not just in music and business. It's not that I want to limit myself to what might be called "age-appropriate" behavior, but I'm glad to have different priorities—to be a little wiser.

This is probably why people come up to me all the time and say things like "You inspired me to become a doctor" or "You got me through a troubled time in my life." I met a man recently who told me he was a two-time cancer survivor. What got him through the days when he couldn't get off the sofa, he told me, was listening to KISS. I would like to think that we all can inspire one another to become the best we can be, to fully realize who we are, by seeing how others have done it. We can emulate the passion and determination and apply it to anything in life.

Part of what's so difficult for most of us is feeling that we're alone in our struggles. But if we open up to the right people, we find out there's actually a lot of support around us, because we're all dealing with the same stuff. When we idolize someone, we tend to see that person as perfect, and I'd rather people look at me and realize that where I am today didn't come without a lot of hard work, pain, and defeats.

Do I have it all? Yeah, I really do. I have the satisfaction of a great job and a great family, and they enhance each other. But anyone can have it all. People compromise; too often they surrender and settle in relationships, in jobs—in life. But the truth is: we can have it all. And we owe it to ourselves to at least try.

I want everybody to succeed.

The top of the mountain is really big. There's room for everyone.

Just remember that our stories never end—your story never ends. At some point it simply gets added to someone else's and passed forward to be told again. It's up to you to make sure you love yours.

ADDENDUM

Life can and should be an adventure of discovery, and for me what makes that possible and what it all comes down to is family. And by that I mean both actual family members and those people we embrace as such. My growth and self-awareness over the years continue to be reflections of my interactions with and support from those people I am fortunate to have placed around me. I would be remiss and perhaps undeserving if I weren't to understand how deeply rooted together Gene and I are. True love and true friendship are built over years of action and reaction. There is no substitute for time, and time does tell all. When I had my first operation to rebuild my ear from rib cartilage, Gene flew up to see me in the hospital—despite an intense fear of flying at the time. When I was separated from my first wife and didn't know where to go, Gene opened his home to me without hesitation, and I lived there for months. He paid for a big surprise birthday party when I turned sixty-one but didn't want me to know. The list is endless. The depth of our relationship, too, is endless.

When Evan, my first child, was born, the very first person I admitted into the delivery room almost immediately was Gene. He was that important to me. In 1994, during a very strained time between us when we were barely speaking, Los Angeles was rocked by a large, damaging earthquake. Regardless of our personal situation at the time, once I recovered from the initial shocks, the first person I called to see whether he was alright was Gene.

We continue forty-nine years later to enjoy each other and annoy each other. He is now a happily married man with a family that years ago wasn't remotely on the horizon for him, nor did it hold any attraction. But isn't that what makes life so rich and exciting? We never know what the future holds, but we are transformed by being open to possibilities that allow us the opportunity to rise to them.

Do Gene and I bicker? Sure. Do we disagree? Of course. It's all small and vastly inconsequential given what we have, what we share, and what we have built.

I don't understand some of what Gene does. I don't agree with some of what Gene says, but time tells all, and I am blessed that he has been such a pivotal person in my life—and that I was smart enough to realize it.

I know many people. Those I consider my true friends I can count on my ten fingers—which brings me to those I love. I can count them on those same ten fingers and still have some to spare. Thankfully, for me, Gene is right there with my family.

I believe that if we don't know that we are blessed, then we don't deserve to be.

Life's potential becomes so much richer and more meaningful when we embrace the blessings we have been given and come to discover the endless ones that are in fact there for our taking and others for our making.

Onward.

ACKNOWLEDGMENTS

First and most importantly I want to acknowledge my never ending thanks to my incredible wife, Erin, and the four most amazing children I could ever have been blessed with . . . Evan, Colin, Sarah, and Emily. You are all my soul and the center of my life and without you, all else crumbles.

There are far too many people to acknowledge without my inadvertently leaving some out, so I will make this very brief.

My collaborator, friend, and partner in both *Backstage Pass* and *Face the Music*: Tim Mohr.

My literary agent and sounding board for both of my books: Roger Freet.

My editor at HarperOne: Hilary Swanson.

My publicity team: Suzanne Wickham at Harper and Kristen Foster at PMK.

Last and certainly not least, those of you who have bonded with me on this adventure through my music, my art, my work in the theater, and my writings. My deepest thanks to you for your encouragement and support. I have that same faith in you and believe we can all be more tomorrow than we are today. Find your true power by freeing yourself of secrets and only look behind you to see how far you've come.

We will meet again.

ABOUT THE AUTHOR

With his first book, *Face the Music*, Paul Stanley added another accolade to his long and illustrious list of artistic accomplishments: *New York Times* bestseller. Stanley cofounded the band KISS in New York City in 1973 and has served as its frontman and rhythm guitar player ever since, as well as designing numerous KISS album covers, costumes, and concert sets, and writing many of the band's biggest songs. KISS has more gold-certified albums than any other American band in history and has sold more than a hundred million records worldwide. Stanley and his bandmates were inducted into the Rock and Roll Hall of Fame in 2014. A successful painter, his art commissions and acquisitions exceed $10 million in sales, with pieces often presold to collectors worldwide. Stanley is a solo musician, the leader of the band Soul Station, a founding partner in Rock & Brews restaurants, and an avid supporter of philanthropic causes such as the Wounded Warrior Project. He resides in Los Angeles with his wife, Erin, and four children.